BIBLE
COMPARATIVES

BIBLE
COMPARATIVES

R. Earl Allen

Foreword by Kenneth Chafin

Word Books, Publisher
Waco, Texas

Dedicated
to
CARL BATES
KENNETH CHAFIN
FRANK JUNELL
because of Proverbs 27:10

Foreword

Earl Allen is living proof that a man may combine the schedule of a busy pastor and the discipline of writing.

Earl Allen is first and foremost a pastor. His love for individuals and his capacity to be moved by their needs is evidenced in all he does.

His preaching reflects wide reading and careful preparation. He is a master both at illustration and alliteration. He anchors his ideas in the Bible and illustrates them from life.

I commend this book from my dear friend.

Kenneth Chafin
Houston, Texas

Preface

Bible Comparatives has been an intriguing study. The comparatives have required the second look but have been rewarding to the author. They are shared with the hope that they will cause others to make a more significant study. These devotionals are purely inspirational in nature and were written for encouragement.

I freely acknowledge my debt to many for their help. My friend Ken Chafin has been most kind in writing the Foreword. The greatest compliment is that Word Books is the publisher for these messages. My sincere gratitude to Jarrell McCracken, publisher; Floyd Thatcher, vice president and executive editor; and Mary Ruth Howes, senior editor; for their encouragement. To my associate Gordon Dutile, who is great in heart and mind, I am truly thankful. My deep appreciation is owed to Nancy Bagby, Arline Harris, and Barbara Brian for seeing these pages through the journey from the pulpit to the press.

R. Earl Allen

Contents

"Behold, to obey is better than sacrifice" (1 Sam. 15:22).

1
Something Superior

Can you stand success?

Few men can endure the constant glare of success without suffering a dimming of their personalities. In success certain warning signs emerge which are fatal to ignore. Victories may be dangerous if they blind us to the stumbling stones that lie in our path. We may win a fiery battle, only to lose a cold war.

The disturbing question of success haunted the life of Saul, the first king of Israel. The end of his tragic story is in 1 Samuel 31, where he sought disgraceful death rather than capture. He failed to cope with success. He didn't heed the distress signals of his disturbed mind, his jealous temper, and his impatient heart. He was quick to give orders but he would not obey them, even when he knew they came from God.

Perhaps his life can best be summarized in three words: his *opportunities*, his *offenses*, and his *obedience*.

11

Saul's Opportunities

No man ever had a finer beginning than Saul. There are many things in his background that are admirable. He lacked no advantage, no opportunity. If it is true that a man is judged in the light of his opportunities, then Saul should have been a great man of God. His abilities were, after all, God-given! Let us look at some of those opportunities.

Israel had been claiming for some time a desire to have an earthly king. Until now, Samuel had been the people's ruler. He was the prophet of God, a ruler of theocracy—"God-rule"—that had existed in Israel until this time. But Samuel was growing old, and the people wanted a king, just as their neighboring countries had kings. Because of the cry of the people God finally permitted Samuel to anoint Saul.

There were many wonderful things about Saul. Physically, he stood head and shoulders above all the others. The Bible says that he had a nearly heroic beauty. The people felt certain that he was the one they desired to be their king. But physical appearance was not enough. Later, in connection with the choice of David as king, God told Samuel, "For man looketh on the outward appearance, but the Lord looketh on the heart" (1 Sam. 16:7).

Saul also had personality, that indefinable, intangible quality so necessary in life and so much in demand in leadership.

He had good judgment. Judgment is something that cannot be taught or explained to another. If one doesn't have it, he probably will never acquire it; but Saul did have the capacity for judgment. He could go into a group of people and organize them efficiently; he could train a great standing army; he had the good sense and the know-how to lead.

In addition to his physical beauty, personality, and good judgment, Saul was fortunate to have a good family and friends. These are the greatest blessings a man can have. His son Jonathan was wise and just in his judgments, and fought gallantly beside his father in battle. And Samuel was the kind of friend who, when Saul was in trouble, prayed all night for him. In fact, one of the problems of Samuel's life as a prophet of God was that he was so close to Saul that it was difficult for him to obey God's command and to reject Saul, despite his disobedience. Friends of this nature are few.

With such advantages as these, why did Saul fail?

Saul's Offenses

For one thing, Saul lost his humility. In his youth, the king had been a modest man. But those days were past. After he had been king for a number of years, Samuel had to remind him, "When thou wast little in thine own sight, wast thou not made head of the tribes of Israel . . . ?" (1 Sam. 15:17). What Samuel was saying was, "Saul, I remember when you were humble before God, when you plowed in the fields and didn't do it to make a good impression but felt it was the kingly thing to do! You worked side by side with your people to ease their burdens. Remember when you were humble before the people and when they were ready to choose and crown you, you hid among the packages and bottles and

13

said you were not worthy to be crowned king! I remember when you were small in your own sight."

Was there ever a more effective way of communicating a point? Saul was able to understand that Samuel was saying, "Saul, you were great when you were little in your own sight, but you are small now because you feel that you have become great." Saul had lost his humility, and this was one of his offenses.

There were others. After he had been king for two years, Saul gathered together a band of two thousand men and went to do battle against the Philistines, an old and mighty enemy. Samuel told him to wait at an appointed place for seven days until he, as God's anointed prophet, could come down and make an offering.

Saul and his small band of men waited, but at the end of seven days Samuel had not come. The Israelites were fearful. Within view was the enemy, thirty thousand strong. Each time Saul counted, a few more of his own soldiers had fled. The eighth day came and, on the other side, the enemy seemed to be gathering strength while his own force seemed to be growing smaller. Saul panicked. He went out to the altar and, in the place of Samuel, the priest of God, he offered up a sacrifice. Saul sacrificed, but he didn't obey.

Saul's offense was twofold here. First, he forgot that his strength was not in numbers but in God. He might well have remembered the prayer of Gideon and the instructions of God to Gideon when he told him that he had too many numbers—"the people with you are too many" (Judg. 7:2, RSV). But men have never ceased measuring things in numbers. If there is any prayer we ought to pray today it is the prayer, "Save us from the nonsense of counting numbers." The strength of the church is not in the number of its membership, but in Jehovah God. God will not have it otherwise. When the battle is won, he wants us to remember that it was on his strength that we depended to fight.

Saul's second offense here was his appointment of himself to make the offering. Old Testament life cannot be fully understood without understanding the role of altar sacrifice. For the Hebrews, such was the only access they had to the living God. Samuel had been anointed by God to present the sacrifices for his people. Saul's sacrifice was unacceptable, not in itself, but because it had not been made in the manner commanded by God. Saul sacrificed, but he didn't obey. And disobedience is the mother of all sins. Its seed bears fruit and multiplies. It produced sin in the lives of our first parents, Adam and Eve; it produced sin in Saul's life; and it produces sin in each of our lives today.

Saul's next sin of disobedience came when he was commanded to gather together the children of Israel and destroy the enemy of God. The Amalekites were descendants of Esau. When the Israelites had entered the Promised Land, these were the people who had dogged their steps all the way. And God said, "Now go and smite Amalek and utterly destroy all that they have, and spare them not; but slay both men and women, infant and suckling, ox and sheep, camel and ass" (1 Sam. 15:3).

Pride interfered, and once again Saul disobeyed God. The king of Amalek, Agag the fiery one, was such a capture that Saul couldn't resist bringing him back, a

15

rope around his neck, and saying to the people, "See what I have done!" Nor could he resist saving the best of the spoils.

To one who has died to self the trophies of grace are enough, but those who live by the flesh have a false pride that urges them to say, "See what I have done."

When Samuel went down to meet him, Saul greeted him, saying, "I have performed the commandment of the Lord" (1 Sam. 15:13). But Samuel heard the lowing of oxen and the bleating of sheep in the background. "That's strange. You tell me that you have kept the commandment of God. If that is true, explain to me the bleating of the sheep, the lowing of the ox." Saul was ready with an explanation. "The people are responsible," he suggested. "They wanted the sheep and the oxen to offer as sacrifice."

Under Levitical law, the sheep and oxen were "devoted" to God, and those belonging to the enemy were "under the ban." Animals under the ban were not acceptable to God as offerings. But Saul had reasoned that if he sacrificed the plundered animals to God, he could keep his own. Thus his explanation to Samuel was a lie. Worse still, he was attempting to shift the blame. Such a remark showed Saul's unwillingness to take the responsibility for what he had done. A king is responsible for the acts of his people; they do not give the orders, they obey. Saul should have known that it was useless to lie or make excuses.

We can always be sure that somewhere in the background there will be the bleating of the sheep and the lowing of the ox! God's divine judgment will always have a witness. There was no one to witness the murder of Abel, but the Bible tells us that Abel's blood cried out from the ground (Gen. 4:10). There will always be the cock crowing, the sheep bleating, the blood crying from the ground. "For whatsoever a man soweth, that shall he also reap" (Gal. 6:7).

God will not be mocked—with lies, with disobedience, or with excuses. He demands total obedience from his servants.

Saul's Obedience

When Samuel rebuked Saul for his action and told him that God intended to deprive him of his crown of leadership, Saul recognized his wrong and apologized immediately. As Samuel started to leave his tent, Saul, pleading with him, grabbed desperately at Samuel's cloak and tore it.

Doesn't this sound like genuine repentance, we ask? It does perhaps at first glance—until we realize that Saul, as we all are, was willing to repent and offer partial obedience as long as it was convenient. He didn't mind being dishonored before God in disobedience, but he had become a proud man and didn't want to be dishonored before his people. He wanted God to overlook his wrongdoing. Surely the Lord wouldn't deprive him of his kingship simply because he had kept the spoils of war. Surely one sacrifice on the altar was as good as another!

Saul wanted to give only partial obedience. It seemed he wanted to trade out with the Lord, saying, "I'll obey you a little bit. I'll go a little way with you." He had fought and won the battle; wasn't that enough? Couldn't God overlook the rest? But God does not accept compromises or "deals."

17

In English history there was a Scot who was ambassador to Prussia for Great Britain. Sitting in on a conference with the king of Prussia and others who were discussing the threat of war, the Scot said, "England, by the help of God, will stand by Prussia." The French ambassador, an infidel, turned to the king of Prussia and said, "God? I didn't know you had any allies by the name of God." "God," the Scot replied, "is the only ally England has to whom she does not send subsidies!"

We cannot buy God. We cannot obligate him. We cannot sell and trade with God at a bargain counter. God's judgments are firm.

Obedience, God said, is better than sacrifice. Actually, obedience is itself a sacrifice, far more difficult than the presentation of a bullock on the altar. For us, bringing an offering each Sunday can become as easy and as ritualized as had the bringing of a lamb for the Hebrews. Often no sacrifice at all is involved. It is far more difficult to tame a rebellious spirit and lay it at God's feet; this is the supreme sacrifice. Total obedience to God's commands involves us wholly—our hearts, our minds, our motives! And obedience makes us a part of the fellowship of suffering with God, who laid his own flesh on the altar. Just as it is far better for the child to obey his parent than to disobey and apologize later, so it is better for us to obey God. We may say we are sorry later, but as with Saul, some wrongs cannot be undone with an apology.

After God rejected Saul as king, his disposition and lot worsened. Samuel, Saul's friend, wept over him. One of the saddest hours of the prophet was spent weeping over a disobedient people. As David, who was to be the next king, found favor with the people, Saul grew more and more envious. Eventually he became so filled with hatred that he tried to take David's life and finally his own. Three times he tried to take his own life: first, by asking his armor-bearer, who refused; second, by attempting to destroy himself with his own sword; and finally, by asking one of the Amalekites to kill him. The third time he succeeded.

I went one day to the home of a woman who had called me, weeping and asking for counsel. As we sat and talked, I recognized a familiar story. She pointed to many priceless objects around the room and said, "These gifts are not symbols of love . . . they're symbols of drunkenness and lost weekends."

Are our gifts to God symbols of love or weak apologies for disobedience?

God said to Saul that "obedience is better than sacrifice." Listening to God is better than giving a million dollars. Jesus saw the insincere sacrifices of his day and said the same thing. "Outwardly, your gifts are in order," he told the priests and leaders, "but in your hearts you are like whitewashed sepulchres." Paul instructed the early Christians that before they brought their gifts to the altar, they should consider whether they had first given themselves.

Albert Schweitzer went to interior Africa as a missionary. With his tremendous medical and musical talents, he could easily have rationalized, "Lord, if you will let me stay here, I could earn enough to pay for six doctors to be sent in my place." He might have provided more money that way, but he would never have had as much influence.

Obedience is better than sacrifice. Paul summed it up

in immortal words when he said, "I beseech you therefore, brethren, by the mercies of God, that ye present your bodies a living sacrifice, holy, acceptable unto God, which is your reasonable service" (Rom. 12:1). Nothing else will substitute. Partial obedience won't do. Complete surrender is what God demands, and it is the only thing that will bring happiness.

The superlative sacrifice is the sacrifice of self on the altar of obedience.

"For wisdom is better than rubies" (Prov. 8:11).

2

Richer than Riches

If you were seeing a display of precious stones, it would be difficult to decide what could be more precious than a ruby. Stimulated by the attraction before you, you might think of some other stone of greater value, such as the diamond. After all, isn't it often said, "Diamonds are a girl's best friend"?

Some of the wisest sages of ancient times have dared to deny this sophisticated statement. In Proverbs 8:11 Solomon declared, "Wisdom is better than rubies; and all the things that may be desired are not to be compared to it." Long before this country went on the gold standard, Job rose to say that wisdom "cannot be gotten for gold," nor can it "be valued with the gold of Ophir," nor "valued with pure gold" (Job 28:15, 16, 19). He continues, evaluating various precious stones and metals—the sapphire, the topaz, silver, onyx, pearls, crystal, and coral—only to conclude that wisdom excels all of them in value. All are found wanting when compared with the pricelessness of wisdom.

Many precious stones are mentioned in the Bible. They are used to symbolize many things. Most were thought to have evil powers. The ruby is mentioned six times, and it is unique in that there is no stigma or evil idea associated with it. There are, however, many legends concerning its origin, character, and beauty.

The home of the ruby is India and Burma, and from these superstitious people comes the belief that the light on the inside of the stone is a flame that fell from heaven and is so much a part of it that man can neither conceal nor remove it. So bright is this light that, in one of the monasteries there, a large-sized ruby was placed in the corner where the monks went for prayer, and no other light was needed. But the Bible tells us that God himself is our light, for there is no other light in heaven; there is none needed, for God *is* light.

Just as the color and value of the ruby are determined by the direction from which it is viewed, so also is the preciousness of the "bright and morning star," Jesus Christ, determined by the cross, by which we stand and view him.

Because of its great value on the markets of the world, the ruby has many imitations. Among the most common are the garnet, the Bohemian ruby, and the red spinel. Did you realize that in the crown of the king of England there is an imitation ruby? It is a red spinel known as the "Black Prince ruby." It was a reward given to the Black Prince in 1361 for having won a decisive victory in battle. It was an imitation, but it is still there.

There are many qualities about the ruby that men

would be wise to imitate, but there are some things better than a ruby. For example, in drawing his comparisons, the writer of Proverbs says there are at least two things nobler than a ruby. The first is *virtue*: "Who can find a virtuous woman? for her price is far above rubies" (Prov. 31:10). The second is *wisdom*.

There are only three wisdom books in the Bible: Job, Proverbs, and Ecclesiastes. In the Book of Proverbs there are more than three thousand sayings written by Solomon alone, and he did not write all that are found there. He was the compiler. The thirty-one chapters contain proverbs written by several authors. Still, Solomon is the one known as the "wise king," for when, early in life, he was given that invaluable choice of what he would rather have than anything else, he asked for wisdom. He appreciated the benefits of wisdom and began to set down the proverbs that came to him. Therefore, we find in his book one of the greatest collections of wise sayings on record.

In Proverbs 1 we find a father speaking to his son. In a practical manner he is trying to lead the boy into deeper knowledge, to show him the better way. He is trying to persuade him early in his youth to seek what is uplifting, noble, worthwhile. The first few chapters are devoted to instruction concerning a good home, the good life, the values of good companions. Then, as the writer moves on, we find him searching out the wider things of life, the whole world.

In Proverbs 4:5-7 he says, "Get wisdom, get understanding . . . . Wisdom is the principal thing"! Such instruction on the father's part makes us wonder whether theirs were really the dark ages, and ours the age of enlightenment as we are told. Is ours really an enlightened age? It is an age of technical know-how, of scientific advance, and of a certain kind of understanding known as public relations. But is it an age of wisdom and *human* understanding? Great emphasis is given to "getting along with people," but what about concern for them? Couldn't ours be more accurately described as an age of sophistication, of the blasé, slightly bored, "can't be bothered" attitude?

Wisdom should be much sought after. The more a person studies, the more he recognizes that he does not have all understanding. Job, seeking after understanding, raised this disturbing question: "But where shall wisdom be found? and where is the place of understanding?" (28: 12). Where indeed is the place of understanding? Wouldn't any man seek to know the truth, being aware that without it he is poor?

Better than Wealth

Wisdom is better than wealth, for it is wealth of a more durable quality. It is a more lasting wealth, although it does not guarantee financial success, nor even an aptitude for earning great sums of money.

The story has been told of a group of people who were shipwrecked on a deserted island before the days of radios and search planes. Far out of the path of regular shipping, they knew their existence would be meager until they were discovered. They worked out a plan to maintain their lives until a ship could find them.

They sent search parties out over the island to find sources of food and places for crops, but one of the groups discovered gold. In great excitement they began to dig. Feverishly they worked long hours in the hope of being very wealthy, thinking of all that the gold would buy when they got back to civilization. At last they realized that they might not be found very soon. They went back to plant what grain was left in their stores, but summer was almost ended. Their stockpile of gold could not satisfy the hunger-cries of their children. There was gold in the caves, but there was no food in the cupboards, and they realized the folly of what they had done. What they had thought was wealth was worthless.

Life is like that island, and eternity the water that encircles it and engulfs us. We are as those shipwrecked. God gives us each the opportunity to decide what is wisdom; we must have the intelligence to make the choice.

Wisdom is not only better than gold; it is older. We don't know how old the earth is, but it has a birthday, because God in his providence formed and fashioned it. Gold also has a birthday because it is earthly. But wisdom is older than earth and gold, for wisdom is God, and therefore as old as God. And man, made in the image of God, has this wisdom available to him if he will only seek it.

The statement has been made many times that while money isn't everything, it is way ahead of whatever is in second place. This is the thought of our culture. This is the feeling behind our sophistication. But God has said—and man will find—that there is something greater than gold.

Better than Strength

To some people brute strength is everything. With their own hands they are able to lift this or crush that.

Physical strength is good, for it is God-given, and God would have us to use our bodies wisely. But physical power should not supersede mental power. The latter is also God-given.

Wisdom is better than strength. One man can do only a certain amount of physical labor, but if he will use his mind he may be able to do the work of many men and ease the work of all. He has only so many hours to live, but if he applies himself to the task of inventing or creating something worthwhile, he may go on living long after his three score and ten.

Science has done much both to bless and to blight. It would be hard to evaluate the wisdom of science. The muscle man should not laugh at the egghead in the laboratory, for the scientist may be finding a way to save the muscle man's strength. But while science has provided us with weapons against disease, it has also provided us with weapons of war. Military strength—like physical prowess—should not be the ultimate goal of either a nation or an individual. The ultimate goal of man, Proverbs tells us, should be wisdom; and such is of God. "Wisdom is better than weapons of war" (Eccl. 9:18).

Better than Folly

A third comparison made in the wisdom books is found in Ecclesiastes 2:13: "Then I saw that wisdom excelleth folly, as far as light excelleth darkness." As light is better than darkness, the writer is saying, so wisdom is better than folly. But what is folly? What is wisdom? Job 28:28 says, "The fear of the Lord, that is wisdom."

Throughout the Scriptures we find that wickedness is

the symbol of the foolish, righteousness the symbol of the wise. Yet some still would not believe it: "The fool hath said in his heart, There is no God" (Ps. 14:1). But Paul said that the "foolishness" of God is better than the "wisdom" of man (see 1 Cor. 1:25).

A widely respected man of science was asked by a man interviewing him, "Is there anything in life really worth knowing?"

"Oh, yes," was the reply. "The only fact in all of life *really* worth knowing is Jesus Christ."

Jesus Christ is the way, the truth, and the life. One who does not know Christ is not wise; rather, he has stumbled in the ways of ignorance. He has not come to understanding, to the supreme fact of all knowledge, the knowledge of God. Jesus is God revealed; he is the truth of God, and knowledge of the Good News he provided is the wisdom of God.

Would you like to be wise? Surely all of us want to know the truth. If we desire understanding, we should seek a relationship with him who is truth. How can we know him? By pursuing him in paths where others have found him? By searching the volumes of learned men? Not altogether. We may dust them off, only to put them aside later and say with the Greeks who stood outside the crowd and appealed to the disciples, "Sirs, we would see Jesus. We want to see Jesus for ourselves" (see John 12:20, 21). The experience of others is not enough; you have to know Christ for yourself. And you don't really get to know him until you start sharing him.

Do you want to become wise? The Bible says, "He that winneth souls is wise" (Prov. 11:30). That means sharing Jesus. That is truth in its ultimate sense! That is the greatest wisdom of all. Are we wise in our own conceits, or are we wise in the things of God?

The wisdom of God will make us richer than if we owned all the rubies in the world.

*"He that is slow to anger
is better than the mighty"
(Prov. 16:32).*

3
Mightier than Might

Throughout God's Word we learn that under God's instruction men who purposed in their hearts to do his bidding gloriously took cities under great handicap. You will remember how Joshua moved under God's command and was able to take the city of Jericho against overwhelming odds. Because he followed the leadership of God, the walls fell.

Caleb, one of the original leaders in the taking of all Canaan under God's direction, even in his last years thrilled to the thought of those victories. He went to the people and said, "Give me this mountain," the mountain of Hebron, knowing full well that the cities in the mountains were well manned and fortified, yet thrilling in his heart to the idea of conquest (Josh. 14).

Solomon is in no way speaking lightly of the ability of a man to take a city when he says: "He that is slow to anger is better than the mighty; and he that ruleth his spirit than he that taketh a city." Gideon also knew that truth. When God spoke to him, he was able to overcome the fear he felt within. Following God's instructions in regard to the number and caliber of his men, he won a complete victory.

David was able to rule his own spirit, also. In 1 Samuel 25 we find the story of Nabal, an ungrateful and insulting man, whom David could easily have destroyed. But David allowed the Lord and Nabal's wife to restrain him from taking revenge.

Despite the anguish and suffering which inevitably accompany war, the conquest of a city is often heralded by the revel of drums, the call of the trumpet, the song of the bugle. A noisy celebration of victory is something that all people enjoy.

This is not true of the fight within. When a man is curbing his rebellious spirit, when mind and heart conflict, the struggle goes on secretly and silently. When the man wins a great victory here, others are not aware of it —he is a hero no one knows. The battle for a city may last only a few days, but the battle for self-control, the struggle to achieve temperance and godliness—that battle is never over. It is the endless struggle of a lifetime, and a man's spirit is the constant battleground for civil war between a man's best self and his baser self.

When a man wins in this war he cannot expect to be crowned, for he is a secret hero who must continue his fight. One of the paradoxes of life is that we are conscious when we fail to conquer our spirits, but often do not know if we succeed. And if the other fellow conquers himself, we probably won't know it, but we will surely notice his failure!

History tells us that Alexander, the young, conquering

monarch, the man of careful military strategy and might, was able to control others because he was able to take a city and a country. But when the responsibilities of his own life fell into his hands, he failed miserably. Let Alexander the Great rise up from the dusty pages of history and say with Solomon, "It is indeed mightier to conquer self than to conquer a city."

The Sinner's Anger

The Bible is a gold mine of practical wisdom, and the Proverbs especially are written on a level which we can understand. Proverbs 29:11, for example, says: "A fool uttereth all his mind: but a wise man keepeth it in till afterwards." Each of us knows what the writer is talking about, for anger is a natural human emotion and common to us all. No matter how natural it is, however, it is an expensive luxury in which no man can reasonably indulge! Ben Franklin called it the most expensive luxury in life.

Sometimes we try to defend our tantrums by saying that it is better to be frank, to say what one thinks. The tongue moves with such rapidity that it is able to pass the mind by. James recognized that although the tongue is the smallest member of the body, it is still the most powerful. No one can estimate the amount of unhappiness and violence it has caused, the number of broken homes it has led to, the peace it has destroyed, the hurt it has inflicted between friends. We excuse anger so easily, yet it leads to the carrying of lifelong grudges—one of the heaviest burdens man can carry. This is the anger of the sinner.

Sinful anger can even ruin one's health. Dr. Roy L.

31

Smith once said that a man can no more neglect a temper than he can neglect a fever, for both are symptoms of deeper and worse ills. But if one continues to "throw fits," he will eventually "*have* the fits." Haven't we heard people excuse acts of violence by saying, "I was drunk . . . I was mad . . . I didn't know what I was doing"? In the courts such behavior is known as temporary insanity. Although some would tell us not to subdue anger but to express it freely, doctors have certified that tempers and grudges can make men ill. Often if a man can be kept in a hospital long enough to give up a resentment, his disease can be healed. "Whom the gods would destroy," wrote Longfellow, "they first make mad."

Science has recently carried on a series of experiments in which animals were provoked to anger and then kept in that condition for a long period of time. The results were many and varied, but one effect was loss of eyesight. Could this be what is meant by "blind rage"? Such an experiment is scientific proof of Solomon's statement that the individual who lets anger color his thinking and control him will find his body adversely affected (Prov. 14: 29-30; cf. RSV).

To be angry as the sinner is angry is to revenge the faults of others on ourselves.

The Saint's Anger

There are other kinds of anger, the Bible tells us. There is the anger of the saint. Ephesians 4:26 says that if you must be angry, "let not the sun go down upon your wrath." If you have carried your grievance all day, at least don't take it to bed with you.

But "be ye angry, and sin not," the first part of the

verse says. The way to be angry and not sin is to be angry at sin. This is the anger of the saint. Anger is sin only when it is felt against people, not against causes. Most of the time our anger is directed at men, but anger is righteous when it is coupled with affection for a great cause! "If it be possible, as much as lieth in you," wrote Paul, "live peaceably with all men" (Rom. 12:18). If it is not possible, be angry at the right things.

Thomas Chalmers, the Scottish preacher, preached a sermon more than a hundred years ago which was a classic then and is now. He entitled it, "The Expulsive Power of a New Affection." Such was the power of John Knox when he stood in the pathway of Mary Queen of Scots on the pier at Leith, waving his Bible in her face. She remarked to one nearby, "I fear this man with an open Bible more than any King my armies have ever marched before." Such was the power of Martin Luther when, after nailing his Ninety-Five Theses to the church door, he was asked to recant. With the "expulsive power of a new affection" he replied: "There are not enough popes on earth or in hell to make me recant."

We need to be mad—angry about the things that break the heart of God. Paul advised the Galatians: "If any man preach any other gospel unto you than that ye have received, let him be accursed" (Gal. 1:9). Christianity needs men like Paul who will get angry, but angry at the right things and for the right purpose—angry enough to spend their lives in defense of a great cause.

We need to become angry against the sins of our day. We need to become angry against the secularism and commercialism of our day. We need to be angry as God was against the misuse of the Sabbath.

The Savior's Anger

What does it mean to be angry as Christ was angry? Was it ever so?

Our "age of toleration" has so removed the wall of separation between holy indignation and petty temper that we are restrained even in feeling emotion for great causes. An authoritative word, a patriotic gesture, a word condemning sin brings uncomfortable silence or raised eyebrows from others, and we may hear the comment, "Such behavior isn't Christlike."

Charles Jefferson was right when he noted our reluctance to ascribe certain moods or feelings like anger to Jesus. But it would be well for us to ponder the occasions and motives for Jesus' anger, for he blazed with anger, particularly in the face of insincerity and inhumanity.

There were times when the disciples knew his indignation, as when he said to them, "Suffer the little children to come unto me, and forbid them not" (Mark 10:14). There was also the time when Peter, in his eagerness to protect the Master, implored Jesus not to risk his life by going to Jerusalem. Fighting temptation, Jesus replied, "Get thee behind me, Satan" (Matt. 16:21-23).

But Christ's greatest anger was against wrongdoing. Toward the end of his life the scribes and Pharisees, eager to find something on which to hang an accusation, tried numerous times to trap him. Time was so short; the cross was so near. They had no feeling for him, no love for his mission and purpose in life. There was among them no understanding of why Jesus had left heaven's glory to come to earth. They dogged his steps, hoping that he would do something for which they could condemn him.

Although he had reason to be angry, he answered all their questions and accusations firmly. He was not angry until he saw what they had made of the Temple, ignoring God's purpose. "My house shall be called the house of prayer; but ye have made it a den of thieves" (Matt 21: 13). He overturned the tables of the merchants and moneychangers and threw them out.

God is love, and Jesus, the Son of God, is also love, and because the Son loved us he hated the things in us God hates. He hated the desecration of the house of God.

Like Jesus, Paul knew what it was to be beaten, stoned, and spit upon. He knew what it was to be ignored. He knew the hatred and violence many felt toward the gospel he preached, but he counted them not worth his anger. Their persecution was insignificant compared to what he was fighting for.

What aroused Paul's sternest anger was false doctrine. "If any man preach any other gospel unto you than that ye have received, let him be accursed" (Gal. 1:9). No other way, no other Christ, no other plan—"let him be accursed"!

It is not wrong for us, as Christians, to feel anger, but let us not pervert it, giving way to selfish pride when someone has hurt our feelings. If we are going to be hurt, let us be hurt by a cause that would demand the very best of us. If we are going to be crushed, then let us rise up and be crushed by a cause that is worth dying for.

There is a time and a place for loves and a time and a place for hatreds, and the two do not conflict. Let us be sure that we are consistent in hating the things the Lord hates. Let us be sure that we love the things the Lord loves. Let us give ourselves to the things that he would choose, always being certain that ours is righteous wrath.

An Armenian girl and her brother were being persecuted by the Turkish army. While the brother was fighting fiercely for his own life and trying to distract them so that his sister might escape, she was able to make her way to a wall. As she scaled the wall, she turned and saw the life of her brother being taken. Having looked full in the face of the man who took her brother's life, she went down the wall to safety.

The day came when this girl was acting as a nurse's aide in an army hospital. She had taken an oath that she would help to aid and heal. In the pursuit of her duties she paused one day to wipe the blood from the face of an enemy soldier, and as she looked down upon the unconscious face, she recognized the man who had killed her brother. She felt all of the emotions that any of us would have felt at a time like that. She thought about the oath she had taken, and then about the misery she had suffered. But she had given herself to the Lord Jesus Christ, and there was in her heart the expulsive power of a new affection. Finally, she acted mercifully and went about her work.

Some time later when he was able to speak, she told the soldier how near death he had come. "Why didn't you kill me when I was in your power?" he asked.

"For one reason only," she replied. "I had committed my life to a higher power, and my God would not allow it."

Vengeance is God's, and if we have put our lives in the hands of a higher power, we cannot enjoy the luxury of lost tempers and let the cause of God go begging while we are off on missions of self-pride. When we lose our tempers, we always lose more than our tempers.

He who rules himself, he who is able to conquer his own spirit, he who wins—though he becomes the unsung hero—is mightier than he that taketh a city.

*"For better is a neighbour
that is near than a brother
far off" (Prov. 27:10).*

4
Kinder than Kin

Better than a brother? Is that possible, and if so, who
would believe it?

We were visiting a family in our church membership
who had lost the husband and father. Their next door
neighbor, an older man who had lost his wife not long
before, spoke of his dependence on the younger man. "He
was like one of my own sons," the neighbor said.

Hearing him, we were reminded of a poetic passage
from the pen of Solomon:

Ointment and perfume rejoice the heart: so doth the
sweetness of a man's friend by hearty counsel. Thine own
friend, and thy father's friend, forsake not; neither go
into thy brother's house in the day of thy calamity: for
better is a neighbour that is near than a brother far off
(Prov. 27:8–10).

Solomon is comparing two "goods" here, saying that

only a friend is better than a brother in adversity, if the friend is nearby.

Over the years much has been written on the subject of friendship. Cicero wrote that "friendship is the only thing in the world concerning the usefulness of which all mankind agrees." Book VIII of Aristotle's *Nicomachean Ethics* deals with the meaning and sacredness of friendship. And not many years ago Sam Walter Foss captured our attention and appreciation with these words:

> Let me live in my house by the side of the road
> And be a friend to man.

But less is being penned today concerning the principle of friendship. Perhaps it is because we do not live in a neighborhood society as we once did. There was a time when, if the cabin or barn burned down, people would have a log rolling or a barn raising. The people would jointly build back what had been lost. The popular song of some years back, "Dear Hearts and Gentle People," describes that kind of society and the sort of feeling it generated in those who shared it. Those people "will never ever let you down."

But the world has changed since then. Now we practically buy in insurance the protection that friends once offered us. The interdependence of neighbors is largely a thing of the past. We are protected by the laws of our land. There was a time when our lives centered around the neighborhood or community in which we lived. But now we buy homes that give us tax advantages and live in a society of apartment houses and do not think a great deal about the matter of neighbors. And we have lost something that ought to be lasting; we have lost one of the great treasures of life.

We hear people speak flippantly these days about the number of friends they have. Often these "friends" are no more than mere acquaintances. I hope we will never find out how few friends we have. Life's observations in crises will teach us that we have many, many acquaintances but not many real friends who are like brothers.

Solomon warned: "Thine own friend, and thy father's friend, forsake not" (Prov. 27:10). The longer you have a friend the more reliable you come to feel he is. People who have blessed your father's name are not to be disregarded nor thought of lightly. Fate may choose your relatives, but you choose your friends, and you ought to choose wisely. Friendship is one of the greatest investments—"the best property," Emerson said—of all life. Your choice may have much to do with your accomplishments in life, since the people you associate with may either poison or ennoble you. They will bring out the best or the worst in you, and will certainly reflect on you. "As in water face answereth to face, so the heart of man to man" (Prov. 27:19).

A few miles out of Jerusalem a horse was being driven in a circle as he pulled some type of cylindrical roller which served as a threshing stone to beat upon the wheat. As he moved, the wind would blow the chaff away and the wheat would remain. When the wind was so still that nothing was stirring, a little boy was paid a few pence to come in every few minutes, take the wheat from the threshing floor, and throw it into the air. Even though it seemed that there was no wind at all, the chaff would scatter and the wheat would fall into place. As the wind separates the chaff from the wheat, so misfortune separates "fair-weather" friends from the real ones.

If there is one thing we ought to remember about the

prodigal son, it is that friends who are bought in prosperity will leave you in poverty. When the boy had spent all that his father had given him, there arose a mighty famine and he began to be in want. One of the things he wanted most was his friends, and he had none. There had been those who had gathered around and followed him, who had laughed when he had laughed, fallen silent when he had been quiet. Some had parroted him as long as he had his inheritance. But when he had nothing left to give, they slipped away, and he was left alone.

The most difficult famine of all is perhaps not want of food but of fellowship with friends. And genuine friendships are not forged only in laughter but are welded together with tears.

Companionship

A close reading of Proverbs 17:17 would indicate that Solomon perhaps meant several things when he said, "A friend loveth at all times, and a brother is born for adversity." Naturally, a physical brother is closer to you and has the best opportunity to be your true friend in the most difficult times. Blood ought to be thicker than water. Sometimes, however, alienations come. Then, we should be grateful for those who behave like brothers when we are in distress.

"Companion" is a good synonym for friend, because a companion is "one who is with you." He is one who "loveth at all times," and when adversity arises and necessity develops, he becomes as a brother. Those who are closest to us are those who are best fitted to be our friends, and they may not always be blood kin.

The Bible dwells at length on friendship, such as

existed between Jonathan and David. When Saul's failure disqualified Jonathan in favor of David, their friendship endured. King David sent his messenger to learn if Jonathan had any sons, and there was one—a crippled boy. Jonathan's friends hid him, fearing that David would want to kill the boy since he was the heir by birth to the throne. It was difficult for the messenger to find the lad. Only after great effort was David able to locate him, and when he did he brought him into his own house.

The butler forgot Joseph in prison, but David was a real friend. Real friends never forget.

Communion

Proverbs 18:24 says: "A man that hath friends must show himself friendly." This is a vastly different concept from that which is so popular today of "winning friends and influencing people." Such a concept seems to me foreign to Christianity, for the whole idea behind such a phrase is one of manipulation. To win friends and influence people is to manipulate them into our way of thinking, to use them for business purposes, to get them to conform to our ideals, or to persuade them to find us attractive so that we may be successful.

The Christian concept is not how to win friends and influence people, but how to win friends for Christ and be of service to others. Jesus said that we are to gain friends, not by manipulation or pressure, but by being a friend at all times. Jesus "loved them unto the end" (John 13:1); he laid down his life for his friends.

Perhaps less is being said about friendship today because we have adopted the philosophy of making acquaintances and using people for our own purposes. To *show* oneself friendly does not mean to *pretend* to be friendly in order to make an impression or a sale. It means to be interested and give of oneself. Friendships do not come by our demanding them, but by our giving ourselves to them.

Just as we need companionship, so we need communion. Man is a social being. We are not meant to live as hermits. Communion with others enriches our lives; we are strengthened by our friends. "Iron sharpeneth iron; so a man sharpeneth the countenance of his friend" (Prov. 27:17). Our enemies will permit us to make fools of ourselves, but friends will save us from ourselves. Solomon uttered a great truth in Proverbs 27:6: "Faithful are the wounds of a friend; but the kisses of an enemy are deceitful."

J. Middleton Murry once wrote, "A true friend is a person with whom one feels safe." Safe we are in the arms of Jesus! "Come unto me, all ye that labour and are heavy laden, and I will give you rest" (Matt. 11:28). Safe in his arms we can be at peace; we can be at rest absolutely. Fidelity is a necessity in a friend, for the pain caused by a faithless friend is sharper than the sting of an adder.

The one friend who can always be counted on is Jesus Christ. He is the "friend that sticketh closer than a brother" (Prov. 18:24). The songwriter captured the spirit of this verse in the words "What a friend we have in Jesus." What a friend we have in Jesus! Too much emphasis cannot be placed on this, for there is none like him in all the world.

Commandments

Jesus said, "Ye are my friends, if ye do whatsoever I command you" (John 15:14). We who have been baptized are telling the world that we are the friends of Christ. We are identifying ourselves with Christ. We accompany him into the water, which symbolizes his grave; we rise with him from the water, which symbolizes his resurrection. And by our obedient act we identify ourselves with the cause of Jesus Christ.

Someone has said that friendship is a tender plant that needs to be watered often. Friendship is not just a mutual admiration society; it carries with it certain responsibilities. There were some who said they would follow Jesus, but they didn't. There were some who said they would never leave Jesus, but they did. There were some who made little comment, but who stayed with the Master to the end.

After-dinner speakers who begin their introductory remarks by saying "My friends," mean nothing more than "you are my friends because you are willing to listen to me." But Jesus' use of the word "friend" was quite different. He paid his disciples the greatest compliment that God could pay man when he said, "I no longer call you servants, I call you my friends" (see John 15:15). What a fellowship! What a joy divine! "I call you my friends."

Jesus also said, "If you love me, keep my commandments" (see John 14:23-24). What commands has Jesus given his friends? If we are truly friends of his there are identification marks which we will bear; we will honor the Savior by accepting his challenge to do whatever he commands.

We will remember the Lord's Day and the Lord's house. We will be identified as friends of Christ if we do this, "not forsaking the assembling of ourselves together, as the manner of some is" (Heb. 10:25). The friends of

Christ will frequent his house. Those who are not his friends will dishonor the Lord's Day and will leave desolate the sanctuary of God.

The friends of Christ will love his Word. Do you like to get a letter from folks you love? This Friend of ours has written to us in the Bible, and if we love him we will surely study his message to us.

If we are his friends, we will "love one another," even as Christ has loved us. The quality of our friendships with one another ought to tell people what communion with God is like. We will seek others to meet him!

C. Roy Angell tells the story of a man who lived in San Antonio several years ago. About three weeks before Christmas, as the man was leaving his office building he found a little fellow dressed in rags looking at his new car. The car was shined to perfection. Curious, the little boy began to ask the owner questions.

"Mister, is this your car?"

"Yes," the man replied.

"Gee, Mister, how much would a car like this cost?"

Knowing how children are inclined to reason like their mothers and dads when it comes to money, he answered, "Well, son, I really don't know."

Perplexed, the boy looked at him and asked: "Mister, this is your car and you don't even know how much it cost?"

"No, the truth is my brother gave me this car for Christmas, and I don't know how much it cost." Then, from the lips of the little fellow came one of the most profound statements the man had ever heard:

"Gee," he said, "I wish I could be a brother like that."

But there is more to the story. This man learned that

45

the little boy had a brother at home who was crippled and could not leave his bed. Every night the little boy would take home descriptions of the tinsel and toys on display in the store windows. The man went to the boy's home and got his little brother, put him in the car, and took him out for the first ride of his life.

Don't you wish you could *be* a brother—or a friend—like that?

Jesus is that kind of friend. Often he is the only one who can qualify as such a friend, for sometimes adversities come that even those who love us most are not able to share. But when we walk through the valley of the shadow of death, he is the one that sticketh closer than a brother and will never leave us.

What other religion in all the world would grant communion and companionship with God himself? What other religion would allow a man in his rags of sin to walk with the King of kings? What other religion would take us out of our sins and make us new men and provide us with a Savior who is the Friend of friends? He hungers for our fellowship. "Simon, son of Jonas, lovest thou me?" (John 21:15-17). He is the most faithful friend I know, for he is better than a brother.

*"Better is a dinner of herbs
where love is, than a stalled
ox and hatred therewith"
(Prov. 15:17).*

5

Little with Love

Have you ever read or heard a quotation so startling that you immediately wanted to know, "Who said that?" "Who wrote that?" "How did he arrive at such a conclusion?" Solomon is the author of some startling words: "Better is little with the fear of the Lord than great treasure and trouble therewith. Better is a dinner of herbs where love is, than a stalled ox and hatred therewith."

You will remember that it was Solomon who had the opportunity of asking God for the desire of his heart, and that he chose wisdom. As author of the wisdom books, he speaks with some authority when he advises us what is good and what is better.

Contestants

When he says that a dinner of herbs is better than a stalled ox, he is not only talking about the food on the table. The language is picturesque, but the menu is not chiefly what he has in mind. He is thinking more about the attitudes of those who sit at the table than about what they have on their plates.

It would seem at first reading that these are the words of a poor man who wants to justify his poverty. The Christian who says, "I'm not rich, but I'm happy," perhaps does not understand what real riches are. His life will reveal that he is indeed rich; he need not justify nor apologize for his financial condition. It is not what is on the plate but what's in the heart that determines a man's wealth.

One of our Presidents liked to rise early in the morning and walk the streets of the city. Another liked to walk the streets of the city as the people were going to sleep. I like to think, along with G. H. Morrison, of King Solomon walking the streets of the city, looking about to learn the needs of his people. Perhaps in one area of the city he watches a lone figure trudge home. It is dark. The man has worked a twelve-hour day. He walks slowly because age and weariness have sapped his strength. His step quickens only when he sees a child come out of a dimly lit home, make its way down the path, and call him father. His step grows a little stronger, and there is a radiance about him. Solomon recognizes the sacred relationship between father and child, and he stands back to watch.

He can easily see through the window; in the homes of those days privacy did not exist. He watches the man's wife tenderly set the meager fare of the working man on the table. There is no meat, for no poor man could afford meat in Solomon's day. The standard of living was vastly different from that of our day. Meat was for the wealthy. As Solomon watches the children gather about the table for the late meal of vegetables, he remembers the banquet halls where he has sat. He remembers the guests, who came to dine upon the greatest foods the world could offer, and he thinks how some came merely to impress one another; others because they were bidden and felt it would be socially unacceptable to refuse; still others because they wanted to see who else would be there. And I can see old Solomon shake his head and go away to write: "Eat thou not the bread of him that hath an evil eye, neither desire thou his dainty meats: for as he thinketh in his heart, so is he: Eat and drink, saith he to thee; but his heart is not with thee" (Prov. 23:6–7).

Wisdom is more than the certification of a degree; it is knowing about the world and understanding what goes on about you. If knowledge is anything, it is seeing into human nature and perceiving what goes on in the minds and hearts of others. Solomon understood happiness because he had known unhappiness in the days of his father David's household. He had known sin, murder, hatred, feuding—everything that could bring heartache into a home.

He had known what it was to sit at his father's table and be aware that hatred and murder seethed within the hearts of his half-brothers and half-sisters. More than one had risen up to kill another. Because of this turmoil in the king's house, Solomon could see the happiness around the table of a simple man's home and say, "Better is a dinner of herbs where love is, than a stalled ox and hatred therewith."

49

Choices

It has been said that life is a series of choices. Sometimes it seems that we have to make a choice between two evils. For example, one may be forced to choose between war and loss of liberty. Many young men die on the battlefields, not because they feel that war is good, but because it is less bad than the alternative of living in bondage.

Often, however, we are given a choice between two good things, or between what is good and what is better. At first glance the possibilities may seem equally desirable. We are told that Jesus often visited in the home of Mary, Martha, and Lazarus. Both women did things that needed to be done, but Jesus said of one, when her sister criticized her, "Mary hath chosen that good part" (Luke 10:42).

Few times in Proverbs will you find that the choice is an easy one—a choice between what is clearly good and clearly evil. The truth we are considering here, however, offers a choice not difficult to make. Solomon is asking us to choose between love and hatred. He is saying, Examine the heart; look at the attitudes of those who sit about you at the table, for that which is in their hearts has more to do with good digestion than what is on their plates. The contestants here are not the vegetable and the meat, but love and hatred—the most consistent contestants that will ever be found in the ring of one's heart. Solomon is looking into man. Surely this is as God does. He is saying that hatred embitters the richest feast, but love can sweeten the meagerest meal.

Think of that famous picture of the old man offering a

prayer for his bread and onion and saying, "Thank you for all this and Jesus." Such a man probably has less trouble with his health than he who sits down to a smorgasbord under tension and feels no gratitude. It has been well said, "A 'stalled ox' may delight the taste of a gourmet, but where hatred reigns in the heart, the savory dish will taste like ashes in the mouth."

In his book *Shadow of the Sword,* Robert Buchanan talks about a man who built a chapel of hate. It would not seem unusual in old England to find a wealthy man who had built a private chapel where he could go to say his prayers. But here was a man who had built a chapel of hate, and when he wanted to vent his anger, he would go to the chapel and pour out his curses within the four walls. The idea sounds absurd until we realize that we do the same. We build walls of hatred, walls of prejudice within, and sometimes the walls are so high and so thick that we are not able to see over or around them. In building such walls we are really only punishing ourselves.

Contentment

Of what does life really consist? We have seen that it doesn't consist of what is on the plate, and not in what a man owns. Jesus said, "Take heed, and beware of covetousness: for a man's life consisteth not in the abundance of the things which he possesseth" (Luke 12:15). Perhaps a clue to what life consists of lies in the words engraved on one man's tombstone in a country cemetery: "My wealth consists not in the abundance of my possessions, but in the fewness of my wants."

Actually our desires are often not determined by what

51

we want, but by what other people have. Our world creates images to which we enslave ourselves. Because "they" have a new color television set, we want one. It doesn't matter whether or not we can afford it; we *must* need it if "they" have it. If we would stop to realize how few our own wants *really* are, we might learn how content we could be.

Paul learned this. In Philippians 4:11 he said: "I have learned, in whatsoever state I am, therewith to be content."

Daniel knew it. He said to the king, "If you will just let me have the diet of my people, I will be content" (see Dan. 1:8-16). He preferred his people's diet to the rich meats and wines of the king's table.

Naomi and Ruth came to be satisfied with the gleanings that fell for them at the corners of the wheat fields. The disciples were content in being with Jesus and sharing part of a loaf and some fish. Jesus was so intent on what he was doing that he was content to go without food in order to explain salvation to the Samaritan woman. And when his disciples brought his dinner to him, he said: "I have meat to eat that ye know not of" (John 4:32). Jesus was saying that life is more than bed and bread. Contentment is a state of mind—a condition of the heart, not the palate. Peace is found within, not without.

After listening to his son's entreaties, a father finally gave the boy the expense money necessary for a long trip. His only request of his son was that he take with him a certain envelope and not open it until he reached his destination. After arriving, the boy opened it and read the words of his father: "Son, I did what you wanted me to do because I love you. But neither money nor the move will solve the problem, because happiness is not without, but within. Some changes will have to be made inside before you will be content." Money may buy the land but it won't buy the landscape. "Godliness with contentment is great gain" (1 Tim. 6:6).

John Bunyan, author of *Pilgrim's Progress*, was a poverty-stricken man who spent most of his time in Bedford jail. His family was dying of starvation, for he was unable to earn a living. His blind child asked him again and again to promise the king that he would quit preaching so that he might work and they might eat. The name of the richest man living in London during Bunyan's time has long since passed from man's lips, but we remember John Bunyan today because *Pilgrim's Progress* has blessed an entire world.

"A man's life consisteth not in the abundance of things which he possesseth." A well-laden table will not compensate for a heart heavy with hatred. God is the author of love, and only godliness will bring contentment.

*"A good name is better
than precious ointment"
(Eccl. 7:1).*

6

Noteworthy Name

During the hurried noonday meal a weary waitress was
trying to listen to a little boy and his parents as both
were trying to order. The parents were insisting that the
child have vegetables, and he was ordering a hamburger.
The waitress, having learned that children usually win in
the end, was giving a great deal of attention to the little
fellow. She took the order of the father and mother and
then turned to the little fellow and asked, "Do you want
mustard?" As she went away the little boy looked at his
mother and said, "You know what? She thinks I'm real."

We think that we are real when someone calls us by
name. Our names are sweet music to our ears. To keep
this attitude from sounding egotistical, we may rationalize
and say that we appreciate another's remembering our
name because it is a sign of a selfless attitude in him. The
fact is that we are flattered!

As long as we are going to be remembered, isn't it

better to be remembered by a good name? Solomon does not mean, in the verse above, that precious ointment is not good, for in his day ointment had great value and was usually used only by kings and the wealthy. It was desired for its healing qualities. Those of us who have known the treacherous power of disease, pain, and death recognize that no monetary value is too great to be placed upon something that will heal a loved one. The price does not matter; it is what the purchase will do for the one we love that is important.

Remember the woman who invested most of what she had in an alabaster box filled with precious ointment? She knew that the Master would soon be going from her presence. In preparation for his death she anointed him aforetime, emptying the contents of the vase upon his head. And Jesus said, "Wherever my gospel is preached, the name of this woman will be remembered, for this act will be a memorial unto her as long as the gospel is spread" (see Matt. 26:6-13).

Precious ointment was of great value. What, then, did Solomon mean?

Character Revealed

In Proverbs 22:1 the writer phrases the same thought a little differently: "A good name is rather to be chosen than great riches, and loving favour rather than silver and gold."

Solomon would not have us think that a man cannot have both wealth and a good name. By "good name" he means "good standing." Solomon was writing in Hebrew, and the Hebrew language doesn't have a word for "name" per se. The word he used is Hebrew for "standing," which points up the close association between one's character and his name. He is actually saying, then, that a man's standing in the community is far more important than his riches, ointment, gold, or silver.

I do not know what associations this verse brings to your mind, but I am reminded of one of the first funerals I attended as a child. I do not recall whose funeral it was, but it was in Keller, Texas. I was quite young, and I was standing outside because there was not enough room in the house. Using this passage as his text, the minister made a great impression on me that day. He told the people gathered that the one who had passed away had made the greatest contribution he could make to his sons and his community by leaving them with his good name.

Choices Realized

Not many years ago the individual in trade always kept a set of scales on the counter. He would put whatever you wanted on one side and lead weights on the other. It didn't matter what item you brought to his counter; it would be measured by the same weights.

Almost instinctively, it seems, we have a way of measuring everything by the same standard, of putting a monetary value on everything in life. As soon as we hear of a house, a car, or a job, we want to know how much it is worth. No longer do we think of education as something essential to the development of character or strengthening of the mind; we measure its value in terms of how much more money it will enable us to earn. We weigh it; we measure it carefully.

Sometimes a good name, like precious ointment, does have cash value. For instance, some buyers came to a great business firm in the South and said, "We want to buy your name, your brand. We want your accounts, and we will pay whatever you think your name is worth." The firm, wondering how they could arrive at the cash value of their name, went over their records for the twenty-odd years they had been in existence, added all the money spent on advertising to that spent on good will, and said, "This is the market value of our name." The purchaser paid the price.

But Solomon is saying, If you have to make a choice, a choice between what is good (wealth) and what is better (a good name), it is better to choose the good name. By comparing reputation with something as desirable as riches he is stressing even more strongly the value of reputation.

To actually have to make such a choice would be difficult for most of us. In the *New York Tribune* about twenty years ago, a front-page article indicated that a young man was offered by his aunt what to him was a large fortune—more than $250,000. The only requirement for him to inherit this money was that he be willing, under the rules of the court, to give up his own name and take the name of his aunt. The young man thought a long time about his father, whom he had lost a few years earlier, and said, "Although my aunt meant well, I would rather have the good name of my father than her riches."

A great man of history made a similar choice. Robert E. Lee, grand old soldier of the South, waited out his last days in near poverty. One day some men approached him to offer him an unusual proposition. If he would merely sign a paper, they would not ask him to make decisions nor put in office hours. They simply wanted the use of his name. General Lee took up his cane and said, "I don't have much, but I am not ready to sell my good name to anyone, especially for a product of doubtful repute."

The cynic may claim that a name doesn't mean anything. (You've heard people say, "It doesn't matter what you call me as long as you call me.") But does a number, a label, or some other form of identification really suit just as well? Surprisingly enough, names become labels or tags because they reveal character. How people remember us is not dissociated from our name. Don't we attach certain meanings, ascribe certain feelings to certain names because we have known people by those names who had qualities we either liked or disliked?

How society has remembered people is often reflected in their names. Consider Alexander the Great, Bloody Mary, Peter the Hermit, Richard the Lion-hearted, and Honest Abe. The Bible also has characters who have become famous, or infamous. Would any loving mother name her child Jezebel, Judas, or Ahab?

In the second part of Proverbs 22:1 Solomon mentions the value of "loving favour." By this he means the attitudes other people have toward us. It should make a difference to us what other people think. We cannot ignore the comments of others, for we must give an account of ourselves; we must be concerned about the influence we wield. It is our most prized possession.

When the apostles were ready to look for men to be church leaders, they said, "We want men of good report" (see Acts 6:1-3). It mattered to them what others said; they wanted men of good character whose influence would count for something. And when Paul wrote to Timothy concerning the qualifications of the leadership, he said: "He must have a good report [from] them which are without" (1 Tim. 3:7). Those on the outside must think well of Christians, he was saying, or the faith will never grow.

A minister has the opportunity to hear many things that other people do not. At the funeral services of an esteemed parent, the man's son lingered with me after the rest of the family had left the chapel. As we stood by the silent form of his father, he said a strange and beautiful thing: "Pastor, say a prayer for me that I will never do anything to hurt the name of my father." He recognized that the name of his father was meaningful in that community, and to him it was a sacred trust. The cause of Christ and the name of his father had been so yoked through the years that what could hurt one might easily hurt the other.

We need to return to the time when a man's word was as good as his bond. Integrity was not to be questioned in the collateral that was needed if one wanted to make a loan. Such is not the case now, but a good banker said, "Collateral must be considered in a loan, but so must the good character of the borrower." "Two things there are whereof every man should be especially tender," wrote St. Augustine, "his conscience and his credit."

A sage of Baghdad said to his young son, "Son, when you go to the marketplace, regardless of what you are offered at the bazaars, look at the name of the person who made the article before you buy." Although fewer and fewer articles have the inscription of the maker on them nowadays, the system is approximately the same.

BIBLE COMPARATIVES

Companies market their products under a brand name, and some are acceptable names which carry with them an automatic guarantee of integrity and quality. Wouldn't we like for our names to carry such a guarantee?

Good character is the obligation of the Christian. We may have passed into a time when, unless there is a witness or a written contract, it is just one man's word against another's. But we will always know as we face one another who is telling the truth. The world will never become upright and honest until we as Christians first prove that our names stand for integrity.

There was a time when mothers didn't name their children immediately. They waited. In fact, the Bible seems to indicate that often years passed before some were given a name. Usually the parents waited for some trait, some ability, some attitude to suggest a name.

The Bible also indicates that although a person may be given a name, the prefix is left up to him. Whether he writes good or bad before that name is his decision. Peter—that fascinating disciple of unstable character—was known as Simon until Jesus said, "Thou art Peter, the rock" (see John 1:42; Matt. 16:18). God spoke to Abram and said, "Thy name shall be Abraham; for a father of many nations have I made thee" (Gen. 17:5). Jacob's name became Israel. And Joseph, of New Testament days, was called by his church Joseph Barnabas, Barnabas meaning "one who encourages us by his life."

Someone has said that the Christian has four names: saint, for his holiness; believer, for his faith; brother, for his love; and disciple, for his knowledge. You may not find that your name will be changed by history, but you

60

can be certain that something will be put beside it. Be certain that it is one of these.

Christian Resources

Absalom wanted a good name. He wanted to be remembered, but not for his contribution to God's cause. Since he had no son, he had a pillar built for himself so that he would be remembered (2 Sam. 18:18). To want a good name for glory or prestige can itself be a snare. A long time ago Joseph Parker wrote that a man cannot really have a good name before the world until he first has a good name before the throne of grace. And he cannot have this if his motive is self-glorification.

Those who built the Tower of Babel said among themselves, "Let us make a name for ourselves, for we want to be remembered." And God spoke from heaven and confused their tongues, and they could not understand one another as they tried to build their tower of pride. (See Gen. 11:1-9).

The only way we ought to want to be remembered is as servants of God, as was Christ.

And being found in fashion as a man, he humbled himself, and became obedient unto death, even the death of the cross. Wherefore God also hath highly exalted him, and given him a name which is above every name: That at the name of Jesus every knee should bow, of things in heaven, and things in earth, and things under the earth (Phil. 2:8-10).

When the battle is over the crown may be given to the

61

caesars, but in the end the crown will fall to the Servant, for "at the name of Jesus every knee should bow."

The point is, not to be remembered after we live, but to be blessed *as* we live. The prayers of a good man avail much. They make a contribution to his community. They make a contribution to his church. He is needed in the hour of crisis; his standing is of good report; his influence is a blessing to those with whom he lives. And in return he is richly blessed.

True, his name will be remembered after he dies. It will precede him to heaven and will crown him in glory. And when judgment comes—at a fixed time in the providence of God when all men stand before the throne of grace—this man will receive his reward for the works he has done in the flesh. No man can receive his reward when he dies, for the Bible clearly states that our works follow after us. What we have lived keeps accumulating interest. A name, good or bad, will linger to bless or to hurt the third and fourth generation. Only when God says that time shall be no more will we know what a good name is really worth.

Some men have lived to crush communities and dominate nations. But they will be forgotten when dust is the leveler, and the name that will be remembered is the name that has served—the name of him who has glorified God through patience in prayer, longsuffering in life, generosity in giving, serenity in spirit, and honesty of heart.

*"Sorrow is better than
laughter" (Eccl. 7:3).*

7
Miracle of Mourning

What does the Bible say about laughter and sorrow?

It is better to go to the house of mourning, than to
go to the house of feasting: for that is the end of all men;
and the living will lay it to his heart. Sorrow is better
than laughter: for by the sadness of the countenance the
heart is made better. The heart of the wise is in the house
of mourning; but the heart of fools is in the house of
mirth. It is better to hear the rebuke of the wise, than for
a man to hear the song of fools. For as the crackling of
thorns under a pot, so is the laughter of the fool: this
also is vanity (Eccl. 7:2-6).

As you read Solomon's words slowly in disbelief, then
read them again to be sure you have not misread them,
you hear him say: *Death is better than birth. Mourning
is better than feasting. Sorrow is better than laughter.
The end is better than the beginning.* And you wonder,
Can these possibly be the sayings of a sober mind? For in

these three or four verses one finds numerous paradoxes. What is Solomon saying to us today? What message does he have for us?

We live in an age of make-believe, a world that is artificial, a world with a tinsel attitude. The pill business is one of the most booming industries in this country because so many are unwilling to face reality. Somewhere between the ecstatic state offered by the pill and the melancholy state of the real world, shouldn't there be another place, a middle ground between extremes?

Spurgeon, that great preacher of England, many years ago visualized man as walking through a valley flanked by a hill of mourning on one side, and a hill of mirth on the other. Poets of ancient days believed that happiness was to be found in the *via media*, or middle way. The one who was able to walk and think straight, whose mind was not confused and harassed, who was not tempted to go astray, would find happiness.

But who of us can live in the valley where the ground is always level? It seems to me that there is always the desire, the urge, the temptation to climb one mountain or the other to see what is on the other side. One must experience the throes of despair, the heights of joy; life never remains the same for any of us.

Mirth

Solomon's words are strange to us, for it would seem— if one had to choose between the extremes—easier and more desirable to draw nigh to the house of laughter where there is light and shouting than to the house of darkness and sorrow. In the light of such a paradox, let us consider the words of Proverbs 14:13: "Even in laughter the heart is sorrowful; and the end of that mirth is heaviness."

What is mirth? The dictionary says that it can be an experience in laughter, and there are all kinds of laughter. From history, the Scriptures, and even our own lives we know of that kind of laughter that comes from one who is not rational; it may even be the laughter of the insane. We also know the cruel laughter of ridicule—shrill and offensive—such as the laughter of those who overheard Jesus say that Jairus's daughter was not dead. We know the unkind laughter of those who believe that life is a lark, that nothing is sacred, and that the "eat, drink and be merry" philosophy should prevail. This was the laughter of those who attended Belshazzar's feast. In blasphemy they took the vessels from the temple of God, drank liquor from them, and laughed at the Almighty. They were merely laughing themselves into hell, for the handwriting that appeared on the wall was proved true. The words read, "God hath numbered thy kingdom, and finished it. . . . Thou art weighed in the balances, and art found wanting" (Dan. 5:26–27).

This is not to say that all laughter is wrong. Obviously it is not. The Bible does not indicate that a countenance of sadness means an attitude of saintliness. Even the saints themselves knew this was not so, for during the Dark Ages one named St. Francis of Sales said, "A saint who is sad is a very poor saint!" And Solomon said, "A merry heart doeth good like a medicine" (Prov. 17:22).

There was a quality about Jesus that made the children want to sit in his lap and be near him. And God knew laughter too. Didn't Sarah say, "God made me to laugh"

(Gen. 21:6)? God, then, is the author of that which is holy and good and healthy; and laughter, especially at oneself or as an expression of joy, is upbuilding. When we are able to laugh at ourselves with a gleam in our eye and sympathy in our tone of voice, then God will call us mature.

Still, it has been said that "only idiots and clowns laugh on all occasions." Sometimes even the face of a clown is not all it would seem. A few years ago the most popular clown in America sought release from life because the heart behind the face was extremely heavy. He was merely covering his burden with laughter. Perhaps this was the kind of laughter Solomon was speaking of when he said, "Even in laughter the heart is sorrowful."

Mourning

"The heart of the wise is in the house of mourning," the wise king wrote, for "it is better to go to the house of mourning, than to go to the house of feasting." If you were faced with such a choice, wouldn't you be tempted to choose the house of feasting? Surely you would be drawn to a feast rather than a funeral.

Not that there is anything wrong with feasting. The Bible mentions several feasts. There is the feast when the family sits down together for bread and fellowship—the father providing, the mother preparing, the children sharing enthusiastically. The Passover was a special family feast.

There is also the feast of brotherly kindness, such as Joseph gave for his brothers after their long separation. When Abraham gave a feast of hospitality for three strangers, the Lord rewarded him, for he had entertained angels unawares. The saints also were given to hospitality, and often in the church at Jerusalem, feasts were given where people came as families to break bread and worship. And Jesus, in his most difficult hours, went often to the house of Mary, Martha, and Lazarus for hospitality and fellowship.

Feasts of charity are also mentioned in the Bible. God promised to recompense the just in the day of resurrection for their service to the needy.

All of these feasts are good, and God would have us enjoy them. But the house of mourning, where sorrow and death are present, sometimes provides a better opportunity for God to speak to us. Didn't he tell us that, in the midst of death, we should consider life? (See Amos 5:1-4; 2 Cor. 4-6.) I am always tempted to speak this way at a memorial service, for sometimes those attending are thinking more deeply than they have thought since the last funeral. Their minds and hearts are captive and they are receptive to the words that need to be spoken.

Many things in life that are altogether necessary are not necessarily enjoyable. Solomon said, "My son, despise not the chastening of the Lord: neither be weary of his correction" (Prov. 3:11). It is well that we not drug our emotions with continual laughter. We can learn much from heaviness of heart. It has been said that "an expression of sadness is the token of a wiser mind than the beaming countenance of a continual joker."

With hearts perverse as ours, perhaps it is good that we should be occasionally crushed with sorrow lest we become hardened and forgetful of our purposes in living. A man in another country, a giant of commerce and in-

67

dustry and a leader in government, learned the truth of such a statement. He rose swiftly in power and his aspirations were great. But he fell into disfavor and had to flee. In despair, he thought three times of committing suicide.

Finally, unable to see any acceptable alternative, he decided to go back to his room and write a letter to his wife explaining that intention. But as he walked, he noticed a crude little cross on the ground. He picked it up, crushed it tightly in his hand as a drowning man grasps at straws. That reminder of faith kept him from suicide. Later, a minister who knew him said that never in his twenty-eight years of service had he heard a man petition the Lord to save him as did that man. Perhaps it is true that "we look up better when we are having to lie on our back."

Solomon wants us to see that although sorrow is not sweeter, nor necessarily more moral or more Christian, its lesson is often more effective. It develops personal strength and individuality; it humanizes our affections, making us more sympathetic and willing to "weep with them that weep." It drives us back to God, to prayer, and to the Bible, making us more deeply spiritual. Even Jesus had to endure the cross, and "though he were a Son, yet learned he obedience by the things which he suffered" (Heb. 5:8).

George MacDonald, a Scottish preacher-novelist of the last century, related in one of his books an experience visiting with one of the church elders. A woman who had known a great sorrow said, "I wish I had never been made."

"My dear lady," the elder replied, "you are not made; you are *being* made."

How true this is. In the midst of sorrow God builds compassion and character as they can never be achieved in times of laughter. Sorrow demands discipline, and from such discipline comes glory: "but we glory in tribulation also," declared the apostle Paul (Rom. 5:3).

When the Babylonian king ordered Shadrach, Meshach, and Abednego cast into the fiery furnace, he saw another walking there and exclaimed. "The form of the fourth is like the Son of God" (Dan. 3:25). In tribulation the angel of God is nearby to aid the distressed and to waken the heart of the wicked. Adversity can be a friend as well as a foe, for it may provide us with a vision of the fourth man in the fire.

The psalmist knew this. Had he learned it earlier he would not have had to suffer so greatly. In Psalm 119:71 he said, "It is good for me that I have been afflicted; that I might learn thy statutes."

In a college near Boston, a freshman girl registered with high hopes. She wanted to learn, to achieve, and to enjoy her education. But paralysis struck her down. For the next five years she battled with braces, trying to learn to walk. After this she finished her bachelor's degree, then her master's, and finally earned her doctorate. She married a Baptist minister and authored four books that have blessed the world. In an autobiography called *These Trembling Years,* she told the story of her fight to learn to walk, confirming the truth of Solomon's words that "the heart of the wise is in the house of mourning."

Sometimes you don't have a song until you start singing in the shadows.

"Even unto them will I give . . . a name better than of sons and of daughters"
(Isa. 56:5).

8
Finer than Family

There are many kinds of shadows in people's lives. Some of them seem permanent.

Charles Wesley, famous English hymn-writer, was suffering under some very depressing circumstances. Feeling the need for special consolation and grace as he contemplated his troubles, he sat at his desk beside an unscreened window in the countryside.

A small bird flew headlong through the window and struck him in the chest, startling him. It scrambled under the large lapel of his coat and he could feel the fast-beating heart palpitating against his own. Quickly he put his hand over the coat and the quivering creature, then looked out the window to see if he could find the reason for its obvious terror.

Nearby a huge hawk circled.

Ah, that was it! The fledgling bird sought safety.

Still holding the bird tenderly against his broad chest,

Charles Wesley saw in its action a picture of his own search for refuge with God in the time of trouble.

He promptly wrote down heartfelt words that thousands of people have sung repeatedly for comfort down the centuries since:

> Jesus, Lover of my soul,
> Let me to Thy bosom fly,
> While the nearer waters roll,
> While the tempest still is high!
> Hide me, O my Saviour, hide—
> Till the storm of life is past;
> Safe into the haven guide;
> Oh receive my soul at last!

The Lord has comfort for every troubled soul, even those who feel their particular heartaches are unique. In the Old Testament we find a word from God to a small class of people—those who were hopelessly childless. In the Bible we read of several women who were childless— all of whom are remembered because their prayers were answered. But a certain kind of man had no hope at all. For him, fatherhood was impossible, and the physical, emotional and social consequences doomed him to chronic unhappiness. God's word for such a man is written out in Isaiah 56:3-5: their curse of childlessness, their conditions for cure, and their crowning covenant.

The Curse of Childlessness

Eunuchs were individuals who usually suffered deep distress. Such a man had upon him the curse of childlessness, which was a particularly heavy personal and social

71

burden in that time and nation. It was an irreversible sorrow, but the Lord promised cure and comfort.

Childlessness may not seem a problem to many. For some families, children are unwanted—they just happen along. Others plan their childbearing. Then there are those who cannot have children, although they want them. Today, legal adoption has helped take care of that situation.

But to understand fully the impact of this passage in Isaiah we must get behind its context. We must look through the eyes of an Israelite at the curse of childlessness. We have to understand how they saw it in order to appreciate the agony it caused.

The first institution God created was the family. He told Adam and Eve to be fruitful and multiply. From that point, the family became of utmost importance. It was dear to man and woman alike. Children were their most prized possessions.

The family was the heart of Jewish life. Everything they did revolved about their family. Their tribal system was based upon it. The land was divided and passed on to the children by inheritance—it was shameful to have it pass into other hands. If there were no children, the inheritance was lost, but more importantly, the name was lost.

Children were considered a gift of God, and for a man to be childless was counted a curse. The Psalmist wrote in Psalm 127:3-4:

Lo, children are an heritage of the Lord: and the fruit of the womb is his reward. As arrows are in the hand of a mighty man; so are children of the youth.

There are several places in the Scripture where the sadness of a home with no children is revealed. Sarah and Abraham were childless into old age. God intervened, performed a miracle, and Isaac was born. They named him "laughter," for he brought a new song to their hearts. No longer did Sarah cringe under the scornful stares of other women.

Manoah and his wife had long been childless when God gave them Samson. Hannah and Elkanah had no child. Then through the grace of God in answer to Hannah's prayer, Samuel was born. Zacharias and his wife, Elizabeth, were also without a child until they were advanced in years. Then John was born, a special gift from God, the forerunner of the Messiah.

In this passage in Isaiah we find a special kind of childlessness—the problem of eunuchs. These were men who had been physically mutilated so that they could father no children. They were considered outcasts. Many of them were thus robbed of their manhood when taken captive by other nations.

According to regulations given in Deuteronomy to govern Israel, a man physically mutilated could not enter the assembly of the Lord. Eunuchs were excluded from the congregation of Israel. Personally rejected and looked down upon, their name would be forgotten at their death. Similar restrictions were placed on illegitimate children; they could not enter the courts of the Lord "unto the tenth generation."

In regard to the interpretation of Deuteronomy 23:1 concerning eunuchs, W. R. Smith says, "Presumably the original sense of this rule was directed not against the unfortunate victims of oriental tyranny and the harem system, but against . . . religious mutilation . . . ."

73

The fact that they could father no children was indeed a curse to such men. They appeared to be rejected by God and left out of God's promise to Abraham, that his seed should be as the stars of heaven (Gen. 15:5), and as the sand of the sea (Gen. 22:17).

It is no wonder that the eunuch should feel cut off from the life of Israel. Sometimes because of an accident, but most often because of the cruelty of despotic rulers, they had been denied the privilege that was treasured so highly—fatherhood. This caused them to say, "I am a dry tree!" No fruit, no successor, no real and permanent share in the hopes of the nation. They were outcasts of the social and religious life of the Jewish people.

Such a situation surely seemed hopeless. This amputation left the eunuch in an irreversible condition. But there was deliverance from this hopelessness, God said.

There were other groups in Israel upon whom God pronounced loss of continuing inheritance. The dying Jacob spoke prophecies concerning the descendants of each of his twelve sons. Simeon and Levi, who had been responsible for a massacre of innocent people, were to be punished for their cruelty: "I will divide them in Jacob, and scatter them in Israel" (Gen. 49:7). The tribe of Simeon was given the southernmost, desert portion of the land, and through the centuries they dwindled in number, moving into the lands of other tribes and blending into them.

But the tribe of Levi redeemed themselves in the eyes of God by fighting on the side of Moses against their brethren who worshiped the golden calf at the foot of Mount Sinai (Exod. 32:26). Although they were literally scattered in Israel, and were given no tract of land as a tribe, God made them his ministering priests: "But unto the tribe of Levi Moses gave not any inheritance: the Lord God of Israel was their inheritance, as he said unto them" (Josh. 13:33; see Deut. 10:8–9).

The eunuchs, also, although their situation was unchangeable, were given opportunity of deliverance from their hopelessness if they would trust God and please him. God declared there was a cure.

The Conditions for Cure

There were, however, conditions for cure that applied especially to the eunuchs. These can be summed up by the word "obedience." The passage in Isaiah gives some specific guidelines.

The first condition given was the necessity of sabbath observance. In Genesis 2:3, God sanctified and set aside the seventh day because he had rested from all his work on that day. The observance of the sabbath was one of the Ten Commandments given to Moses. In Exodus 10:8 we find, "Remember the sabbath day, to keep it holy."

The Lord, through Isaiah, was not speaking of mere token observance. The eunuchs might rationalize, because of their exclusion from the Temple of God, that it was no use for them to try to keep God's laws or worship him, that he, as well as the people, rejected them.

The word "sabbath" means to rest from labor. It is a day to be sanctified and to be kept holy. Even the leaders in Israel, the priests commissioned by God, allowed it to deteriorate into mere ceremonial observance, a condition that was not pleasing to God. When the Israelites went into captivity, God listed that as one of his judgments against them.

Men seldom quarrel with the principle of a day of rest,

but they usually want to observe it in their own way, not in God's way—they want to write their own rules. A day dedicated to God should not be used in a light or flippant manner. To disdain the day which God has set apart is a grave disobedience.

We are to observe the day in reverence. It is attitude of heart that determines whether or not we please God. No amount of ceremonial show or token regard will replace genuine reverence.

The second condition stated in this passage is to choose always to please God. It is one thing just to live life in one's own way; it is quite another to live it in accordance with the revealed will of God. And that is exactly what is meant by "choose the things that please me" (56:4). Man's steps must be ordered by God or happiness will not result. The things that delight God are to determine the lifestyle of those who wish a cure for their hopeless situation.

Too many times we try to compartmentalize our lives. We are willing to allow God to control certain areas, but other areas we want to run our own way. We tell him, "Hands off!" There is little doubt that the Lord lives in rather cramped quarters in many of us. We must realize that he is either Lord of all or not Lord at all.

God wanted the eunuch to submit to his will in all areas of life. The final condition set forth in Isaiah 56:4 was that the eunuch was to take hold of God's covenant. He had certain restrictions, but they should not keep him from God, even in the very area of his problem.

The covenant spoken of is found in Genesis 17:10, and the sign of obedience toward it is circumcision. This was a special pointer toward the "Seed" that should come, and the hoped-for destiny of every child born. The eunuch could not share in this hope as other men did, but that was no excuse for disobedience to God's declared will.

Circumcision itself performed no mighty work or miracle of transformation—no more than baptism effects salvation today. In each case the rite is an outward expression of an inward change and commitment.

In the Christian fellowship, there was no carryover of the Jewish regulation regarding eunuchs. It was truly "whosoever will" may come. In Acts 8, there is an interesting story about a eunuch and baptism. Among the Gentiles, men in court positions were often made eunuchs. In this case we are told that the Ethiopian eunuch was treasurer for Candace, queen of the Ethiopians. Evidently the man was also a Jewish proselyte and he was reading Isaiah with a hungry heart when the Holy Spirit brought Philip to teach him. This faithful evangelist of the early church told the Ethiopian about Jesus' crucifixion and resurrection.

Soon the man made a request: "See, here is water; what doth hinder me to be baptized?" (Acts 8:36).

There was no legalistic qualm in Philip's mind—he knew the gospel was to *every* creature and he replied, "If thou believest with all thine heart, thou mayest." Only the man's faith mattered.

God does not honor pomp or ceremony for their own sake. He is not pleased when our voices claim piety but our lives proclaim sin. Such lives are what our Lord spoke of in Matthew 23:27 when he said, "Woe unto you, scribes and Pharisees, hypocrites! for ye are like unto whited sepulchres, which indeed appear beautiful outward, but are within full of dead men's bones, and of all uncleanness."

Obedient faith is what pleases God most.

A wealthy man was looking for a new chauffeur. To secure the most qualified, he gave each applicant very demanding road tests, which included mountain driving. One of the drivers, to impress his prospective employer with his extraordinary skill, sped along a winding road at high speed, skirting the edge of a precipice as closely as possible. Another applicant, however, got the job.

When the employer was asked why this choice instead of the man who demonstrated proficiency at skimming the rim of the canyon, he replied, "I wasn't interested in which one could come the closest to danger. I wanted a man who would take the safe path and avoid the brink of disaster."

Neither is God interested in how close we can come to breaking his commandments and still be legitimate, but rather how obedient we are to his will.

"He that hath my commandments, and keepeth them," Jesus said, "he it is that loveth me: and he that loveth me shall be loved of my Father, and I will love him, and will manifest myself to him" (John 14:21). God honors the man who trusts him completely and is willing to obey fully. This reward for loving obedience was God's message to the brokenhearted, dejected eunuch who considered himself a "dry tree," cut off from God's blessings.

Children of the flesh are not the only means an individual has of affecting the future of the world beyond his lifetime. One matron who recently retired from many years' service in a children's home estimated that she had touched the lives of more than three hundred boys and girls of all ages. Many wrote back in later years to "Dear Mom" and thanked her for the good training she had given them. One of her qualifications for the job was that she had raised children of her own, but many unmarried or childless women who are schoolteachers and Sunday school teachers, nursery attendants, and youth sponsors, have affected the lives of children and young people in an equally effective way. Sometimes they have the privilege of seeing "children's children" of their early pupils.

The conditions Isaiah gave for a cure of the life of a childless man would not bring a physical miracle to reverse the condition, but was designed to bring the person into a place of usefulness, acceptance, and permanent contribution.

The Crowning Covenant

In Isaiah 56:5, God gave the eunuch promise of a crowning covenant. His promise is truly finer than family: "Even unto them will I give in mine house and within my walls a place and a name better than of sons and of daughters: I will give them an everlasting name, that shall not be cut off."

Can you imagine what these words meant to the eunuch? He was a social castaway. He knew the mental anguish of not having children to carry on his name. He suffered religious isolation, being unable to enter the Temple.

In this crowning covenant we find God promising the eunuch a place and a name better than sons and daughters. God spoke of his kingdom. It is not a reference just to the earthly Temple, but rather to the eternal heavenly reward. Here is a promise that the eunuch, who had been tormented by realization that his earthly name would perish at his death, could gain a name everlasting, one that would never be cut off.

Faithful obedience will be rewarded; that is stated

very explicitly near the end of the Bible. "Blessed is the man that endureth temptation," wrote James, the Lord's brother, "for when he is tried, he shall receive the crown of life, which the Lord hath promised to them that love him" (Jas. 1:12). The Lord promised the same thing to the believers at Smyrna: "Fear none of those things which thou shalt suffer: . . . be thou faithful unto death, and I will give thee a crown of life" (Rev. 2:10).

In a former generation, the great name in evangelism was Billy Sunday, who held massive crusades all across the United States. For seventeen years his children's worker was Miss Frances Bennett, a Bostonian who started out in Y.W.C.A. work. She spoke to multiplied thousands of children and many were saved. A favorite verse of hers was Isaiah's word directed more exclusively to women: "Sing, O barren, thou that didst not bear; break forth into singing, . . . for more are the children of the desolate than the children of the married wife, saith the Lord" (Isa. 54:1).

Miss Bennett spoke with confidence of the "crown of rejoicing" promised by the Lord to soulwinners, according to Paul: "For what is our hope, or joy, or crown of rejoicing? Are not even ye in the presence of our Lord Jesus Christ at his coming? For ye are our glory and joy" (1 Thess. 2:19-20). She considered this prospect finer than family.

Many other men and women, though blessed with no earthly seed, have striven for God's crowning covenant. Throughout the Bible God's people are admonished to seek riches laid up in heaven, fruit that will not pass away but last forever—and all the people any Christian has touched for God will be there as living testimonials.

Meeting God's conditions results in God's blessings. "The righteous shall be in everlasting remembrance," says Psalm 112:6.

On this earth, men live and die and are usually forgotten in the passage of years. Most of them have families to carry on their blood and their name. Sometimes it is an inheritance to be proud of, but other times it is not. No matter which—it only lasts for a while. But God gives those who are faithful to him a name that is better than sons and daughters. Nothing compares to having your name written in the Book of Life and, even more than that, the possibility of hearing God's "Well done, thou good and faithful servant."

The account of Spurgeon's conversion is familiar, but one thing I miss is the name of the illiterate shoemaker God used. In great agony of soul, Spurgeon attended a little Methodist chapel one Sunday morning. Because of a severe snowstorm, the minister was not there. An uneducated shoemaker tried to expound on the text, "Look unto me, and be ye saved" (Isa. 45:22).

After floundering a while, he suddenly pointed in Spurgeon's direction and shouted, "Young man, look to Jesus Christ!"

That did it! The man who was to become the "prince of preachers" was saved through the simple admonition of that now-forgotten shoemaker. When we get to Heaven, we will find the name recorded there—no doubt, *finer than family!*

81

*"It is better for thee to
enter into life maimed,
than having two hands to
go into hell" (Mark 9:43).*

9

Prudent Pruning

When we think about physical amputation, something within us revolts. The loss of a limb or an eye seems a cruelty too great to bear. Thus, when we hear Jesus say, "If thy hand offend thee, cut it off . . . . if thy foot offend thee, cut it off . . . . if thine eye offend thee, pluck it out" (Mark 9:43-47), we have difficulty accepting the harshness of such words. We find it much easier to understand the gentle Jesus who said, "Come unto me, all ye that labour and are heavy laden" (Matt. 11:28). Severity and harshness of tone we think of as alien to a merciful Savior, and we ask with the disciples, "This is an hard saying; who can hear it?" (John 6:60).

There were other times when Jesus spoke harshly, as when one who wished to follow him came and said, "Lord, suffer me first to go and bury my father," and Jesus replied, "Follow me; and let the dead bury their dead" (Matt. 8:21–22). It wasn't easy to be a believer. Often

82

the disciples followed without understanding Jesus' words. Jesus realized that, although the multitudes listened spellbound to the beatitudes, they would not follow when times became difficult. He told them that they must forsake father and mother, brother and sister, to follow him. If they could not do so, they were not worthy to be his disciples.

Hard sayings, indeed, and who could hear them?

Yet, harder still is Jesus' command to pluck out an eye or chop off an arm that offends. What did he mean by such a command?

If we read Jesus' words a second time, we realize that he is talking about the seriousness of sin. "It is better," he says, "for thee to enter into life maimed, than having two hands to go into hell, into the fire that never shall be quenched: where their worm dieth not, and the fire is not quenched" (Mark 9:43-44). He is describing the valley of suffering. The place is polluted and the fire burns day and night. All that can live there is the worm and the fire that cannot be extinguished.

Wouldn't it be better to save part than to lose all? Wouldn't a man trapped in a burning building risk breaking a leg to escape suffocation? "For what is a man profited, if he shall gain the whole world, and lose his own soul?" (Matt. 16:26).

Jesus is speaking here of spiritual amputation, of man's need to cut sin out of his life. A minister tells of being called one morning to a hospital to talk with a young man who had taken Jesus' instructions literally. He had severed his hand from his body because of some sin. He explained, "I have done exactly what Jesus told me to do." Actually he had done far from what Jesus told

83

him to do. His act was only an outward attempt to rid himself of guilt. Cutting off the foot that stomps a man to death doesn't make a man a saint after the foot is amputated nor bring to life the one murdered. Cutting off the hand of a thief, as was done in biblical times, does not mean that his heart will not steal. Plucking out a wandering eye does not assure that the mind will not wander. The hand is merely a symbol of what we do; the foot, of where we go; the eye, of what we see. It takes more than physical surgery to change a man's heart; it takes surgery of the spirit.

Decision

Salvation is God's gift, the Bible tells us, but discipleship is the responsibility of each believer. Each man is responsible for his own growth. Therefore, each man is responsible for weeding out the sins in his life. Until he does so, there will be little growth. Each must decide for himself what to "cut off" or to "pluck out."

"Most of the difficulties of trying to live the Christian life," wrote Henry Drummond, "arise from attempting to half-live it." It is our unwillingness to decide what we can and cannot do that points to our failure. With the prophet of old who stood on Mt. Carmel and said, "If God be God let us worship him, but if Baal be God, let us worship him," let us call for a decision in our own lives.

What did Jesus mean when he said, "If thy hand offend thee"? To offend does not mean to make angry, as it would in our language in our own day. Dr. B. H. Carroll suggests that in Jesus' day it had two or three meanings. The most acceptable meaning was to be a stumbling

84

block. That is, if you were accustomed to walking a given path and suddenly found something in that path, you would have encountered a stumbling block, an obstacle that "offended" you, making it easy for you to fall. You would move it out of your way.

To offend might also mean the placing of an obstruction in your spiritual path that would block your progress in faith. If another puts an obstacle in your way that hinders your worshiping or serving God, then that obstruction will be offensive to God.

Third, an offense might be something that someone put in your way that would make you angry and cause you to sin against the Lord. Jesus is saying, because these things "offend" you, remove them from your life so that they will not influence your personality or conduct. "Whatever sacrifice is necessary to the securing of the main thing," said Dr. Carroll, "that you must make."

Denial

How do we perform this spiritual surgery? First, by denying ourselves. Many great men have found this to be true. "Self-denial is the test of religious earnestness," wrote Cardinal Newman. A great German poet found the first lesson of life to be "Renounce!" Thomas Carlyle was often overheard saying to himself, "Thou must go without, thou must go without." And Paul sacrificed personal success, saying, "What things were gain to me, those I counted loss for Christ" (Phil. 3:7).

Jesus put it most clearly of all: "For whosoever will save his life shall lose it; and whosoever will lose his life for my sake shall find it" (Matt. 16:25). The choice is be-

85

tween self-surrender and the rubbish-heap. We must be the ones to decide. "Denial has to come into your life somewhere," said Joseph Parker. "You deny the body or you deny the soul."

Satan dogged Jesus' steps, taking him to the highest pinnacle and offering him the choice between a worldly crown and a cross, and Jesus made his choice. He took the cross. We must choose also—between self-surrender and self-slaughter.

Discipline

Self-denial requires discipline, and discipline is a personal matter. If life is a vine, we need to do some of our own pruning. We must decide for ourselves what we can and cannot do. Values differ from person to person.

Any true disciple of Christ knows the areas where he must limit himself. No life is complete without discipline, repression of wrong thoughts, constant guarding of natural tendencies. Unless held in check these may, like the vine, grow in all the wrong directions. As David Gregg has said, "Sin as a caterpillar is bad enough, but sin as a butterfly is a thousand times worse."

Many of us are perfectly willing to admonish others, "I think it is wrong for you to do this or that." But Jesus told us to look into our own hearts and examine our own lives. You must decide what becomes a stumbling block for *your* feet, what keeps *you* from the house of God, what keeps *you* from serving the Lord. You must decide what is hindering the will of God in *your* life.

Spiritual surgery can have dire consequences if we try to work on others' lives. It is a personal obligation in our own. If circumstances force us to alter our steps in spite of our resistance, we do not enlarge our Christian lives. We have simply changed course because we were forced to. Often God does that, but we shouldn't wait for God to humble us; we should humble ourselves.

Years before there was commercial travel in a certain area, a missionary went in his own boat to an unreached country. It was cold, barren, and lonely. For quite a while he was faced with the temptation of getting into his boat and returning home. Realizing that this meant he placed love of his homeland above love of souls, he said to himself, "I have to remove this temptation, for the message of Christ is worth more than anything else in the world." He dug a large grave and buried his boat in it, cutting off the outside world and his chance of going back.

What in your life needs amputation? Look carefully at what you are accomplishing for God in your life. Look at what you have and what you want. It is never an easy decision, but would you not say to a surgeon, "If my life can be saved by surgery, then operate. If my life can be saved by amputation, then amputate"? Must we not also face the Great Physician and say, "O God, whatever it is, whether it is the aggressive beast in my nature or the slothful spirit that clings to home fires instead of being out working for God, help me get rid of it"?

Why should we discipline ourselves?

First, for our own sakes. Without discipline we cannot grow, nor can we inherit eternal life. "Sacrifice is not for sacrifice's sake but to preserve life," said J. D. Jones.

Second, we should discipline ourselves for the sake of

others. In Mark 9:42, Jesus said, "Whosoever shall offend one of these little ones that believe in me, it is better for him that a millstone were hanged about his neck, and he were cast into the sea." If our conduct prevents others from seeing the way to Christ, then we are not fit to be called his disciples.

Finally, if we have disciplined ourselves for others' sake, we have done it for Jesus' sake. Who could ask for more?

*"For it were better for me
to die, than that any man
should make my glorying
void" (1 Cor. 9:15).*

10

Rejected Rights

The apostle Paul was an intense individual who found
little time for relaxation. The retreat and loneliness of
prison were not easy for him. He much preferred the
challenge of the missionary journey.

At Corinth there was always a problem of communica-
tion. Somehow Paul never seemed able to get through to
the people there. Many pastors came and went. The people were demanding; they wanted great orators such as
Apollos to speak in their pulpits. The weightiness of
words impressed them. So Paul considered carefully what
he must say to them concerning their obligations:

If we have sown unto you spiritual things, is it a great
thing if we shall reap your carnal things? If others be
partakers of this power over you, are not we rather?
Nevertheless we have not used this power; but suffer all
things, lest we should hinder the gospel of Christ. Do ye
not know that they which minister about holy things live

of the things of the temple? and they which wait at the altar are partakers with the altar? Even so hath the Lord ordained that they which preach the gospel should live of the gospel (1 Cor. 9:11–14).

Paul is not speaking on his own behalf here, but on behalf of his fellow ministers, for he continues:

But I have used none of these things: neither have I written these things, that it should be so done unto me: for it were better for me to die, than that any man should make my glorying void. For though I preach the gospel, I have nothing to glory of: for necessity is laid upon me; yea, woe is unto me, if I preach not the gospel! . . . What is my reward then? Verily that, when I preach the gospel, I may make the gospel of Christ without charge, that I abuse not my power in the gospel. For though I be free from all men, yet have I made myself servant unto all, that I might gain the more (vv. 15–19).

Paul uses paradox here, saying that he is at liberty, yet bound; free, yet the servant of all. He means that the only truly liberated person is the Christian, the man who has been loosed from the penalty of his sins and has made himself Christ's servant. There is no hint of martyrdom in his words, no sense of failure or desire to quit. He is magnificently obsessed with his calling, and one feels certain that his ministry is the most important thing in his life.

Paul is not speaking lightly nor glibly when he refuses financial help from the church lest any should think his motives amiss. He is most serious when he says he would rather die than for anyone to make his ministry empty, void, meaningless. The law of self-preservation is strong, but for one who is already dead—dead to self—the problem does not exist.

Paul spoke about death many times. He had no fear of it, for he had died on the Damascus road. There was a fierceness about his life that stood out as much in his early persecutions of the church as it did in his discipleship. When Jesus spoke to Paul that day, he turned his life over to God. From the moment that he died to self and God offered him life, Paul had but one purpose, and that was to do the work of God. He despised death; it held no peril for him. When you threaten to destroy a person who has already destroyed himself in order to give himself up to the living of the gospel, the threat holds no terror. Paul said, The only glory I have is the glory of Christ; I would rather be physically dead than for anything to happen to that glory.

His reasoning is both scriptural and sound as he talks about the principles involved in receiving annuity for the ministry. He discusses the privileges and problems of those who are called, who must live and eat and work in the Temple. He will not allow the ministry to be discredited nor to go unrewarded because of the smallness of some. He is simply saying, "If you feel that I have come to you for the material things of life—if you feel that these are the only things that I am in the ministry for—it would be far better that I be dead."

Paul is also suggesting that the person who says this is himself already dead because he has lost his sensitivity to the things that really count. He has lost the thrill of the things of God. He has been able to come into the house of God and still not feel the Spirit move. He has been able to sleep through a revelation of God's Spirit, and then walk away and say like Jacob, God must have been here but I was asleep and didn't know it. Paul is saying, When I reach the point where no longer do I thrill to what I am doing, when my ministry is nothing more than a duty, when I preach only because it is eleven o'clock, then I would rather be dead!

In Romans 11:13 Paul said, "I magnify mine office." There were those who ran him out of town. There were those who stoned him. There were those who beat him. He did not have the respect that we in the ministry have had in later days. Yet there was something in him that led him to say, "I magnify or glorify my calling."

Privilege

The present enrollment of ministerial students in our denominational schools—both colleges and seminaries— is not sufficient to take care of the advancing number of churches. What has happened in some denominations is fast becoming a creeping paralysis among all. And though the problem has not yet reached an alarming stage, there are dangerous trends. Perhaps it is because we no longer feel about the ministry as Paul felt about it; perhaps it has become more man's activity than the work of God. Paul always stressed that God had called him into the ministry. It was not the church or the apostles but "the Holy Spirit that made you the overseers of the church" (see Acts 20:28). Ultimately it is always the Spirit of God that calls ministers both into the ministry and into the church where they are to minister.

Colonel Robert G. Ingersoll, whose caustic wit few could match, said some years ago that the ministry is best suited for "a man of religious turn of mind, consumptive habit of body, not quite sick enough to die nor healthy enough to be really wicked." Many laughed, as though the ministry was inconsequential and really didn't matter. But on another occasion, Sydney Smith had a good answer. Speaking on the same platform with Smith, Ingersoll turned to him and said, "If I had a son who didn't have a good mind, I would want him to be a preacher." Smith replied, "I'm sorry your father didn't share the same emotion."

Paul said it was a privilege—a privilege!—to handle the word of God. Spurgeon evidently believed so too, for he once said concerning his own son, "If God calls my son to be a missionary, I pray that he will never settle for being a king."

In southern France where the Roman Catholic Church is predominant, a large recruiting poster was placed near a college where young men would see it as they left the campus. It said: "Birth, communion, confirmation, marriage, and death are the five greatest events in a human life. Wouldn't you like to be part of all this?" These events were, of course, taken from the dogma of the church, but isn't Paul saying something similar? He is saying that in the ministry one experiences some of the most rewarding as well as some of the heartbreaking times of life. In such times there is a great need for God, and oh, that we would have God's man!

One of the most magnificent statements I ever heard came from a man who had ordained more preachers in Texas than anyone I know. He was always poorly paid, and during the depression was not paid at all. There was something about the greatness of this man that penetrated his entire ministry. Although inflation was high at the time of his retirement, he was still underpaid, his retire-

ment income scarcely an existence. When it came time
to honor him, he made one of the greatest statements I
believe I have ever heard. He said to the board of trustees,
"Gentlemen, I want to thank you for paying me to do the
things I would gladly have done free had I been finan-
cially able."

Paul stood that day and said, "The preeminent thing in
my life is preaching the gospel and no man shall make this
void."

Pacifier

There are some who feel that the ministry ought to be
an intellectual platform from which we give forth bits
of wisdom and new philosophy. But philosophy, which
means "love of wisdom," often means merely "love of
words." Often we have preached over the heads of people instead of directly to their hearts. A minister gave a
good piece of advice when he said to a young man, "Son,
don't preach to their minds; some men don't have good
minds. Preach to their hearts; every man has a heart."
Preach to the heart, for some man's heart may be hardened
against God.

Halford E. Luccock, the great teacher-preacher, said
that preachers ought to remember that there are four
trinities: (1) the trinity of heaven—God the Father, God
the Son, and God the Holy Spirit; (2) the trinity of the
Old Testament—Abraham, Isaac, and Jacob; (3) the
trinity of the New Testament—Peter, James, and John;
and (4) the trinity in the church—Tom, Dick, and Harry,
who have little opportunity to know much about God
except as the man who stands in the pulpit communicates
God to them.

Some people, on the other hand, feel that the preacher should be a public pacifier, a good mixer in church and in community groups—a man ready to compromise. But such a man, in the end, will accomplish nothing more than pacifying petty people.

Others try to make the minister nothing more than a social worker. As the number of Jesus' followers multiplied after Pentecost, the Greeks among them were unhappy because the widows of their community were being neglected, they said. The apostles called the church together and appointed seven other men to distribute the food, declaring that they could not "leave the word of God, and serve tables" (Acts 6:2). Their love of the ministry of the gospel of Christ was too deeply entrenched for them to neglect it. Criticism from the membership didn't change the disciples' attitude; it only changed their organizational methods to enable all the work of the church to be carried out.

Perhaps we could learn from their experience. Today it is all too easy to allow the pressures of "serving the church" to distract us from preaching the word. We spend all our time putting out brush fires instead of fanning great flames. Should we as preachers or teachers lead conquering battalions or merely follow community design?

Preacher

It is said about Jesus that he came preaching (Mark 1:14). This was the need of his life, the burden in his heart. And the world needed him.

Because Jesus himself set the pattern, preaching must have preeminence.

We are inclined to think that a minister has to master

his message. In truth, the minister must come to the place where the message masters him. We worry about the consequences "if we do preach," while Paul discussed the consequences "if we don't preach." "Woe is unto me, if I preach not the gospel!" he said.

We use the word *woe* in a casual way today. With only slight provocation someone will slap his forehead and say, "Woe is me." But in biblical times the word carried with it a much more serious meaning, involving judgment.

Jesus used the word several times. "Woe unto you, scribes and Pharisees" (Matt. 23:13). "Woe unto him, through whom [offenses] come" (Luke 17:1). "Woe to that man by whom the Son of man is betrayed!" (Mark 14:21). These are only a few of his uses.

Job, Isaiah, and Jeremiah had also used it in the Old Testament. Therefore, Paul was well-acquainted with its history, and he knew that unless he preached the message that burned within, he would be miserable. In his own desolation he cried out, "Woe is unto me, if I preach not the gospel!" It was the tribunal of heaven that tried him, not the vote of the congregation. In his own soul there was knowledge of the emptiness that would fill a heart that does not give testimony to what it has seen and heard. "We cannot but speak the things which we have seen and heard," said Peter (Acts 4:20).

But people do not always want to hear.

During the California gold rush there lived a man short of stature but great of spirit. When he tried to preach, no one would let him. No one would listen. They laughed at him. After all, they were busy mining gold. Who had time to go to church if it was possible to become a millionaire before dark? Each time he tried to gather a crowd somebody would come into town with news of a strike and the others would be gone; he would lose his audience before his text was read.

When he had stood it as long as he could, he went outside of town, bought a horse, and rode into town as the lucky prospectors had done hours before, shouting at the top of his voice: "I have good news! Good news!" He rode the horse the length of the street and back again, and when the crowd was gathered, he sat there on horseback, opened his Bible, and read, "For unto you is born . . . a Saviour" . . . the greatest news in all the world!

The preacher is the bearer of good news—one who "desireth a good work" (1 Tim. 3:1). It is his responsibility to stretch the mind, touch the heart, tan the hide, and provoke the will. If he is able to accomplish these things, then the message has indeed mastered him. Paul was willing to die to do it.

*"For it is better ... that
ye suffer for well doing,
than for evil doing"
(1 Pet. 3:17).*

11

Risk of Righteousness

Ever since Job's time, philosophers have been raising the question, Why do men suffer? If God is good, why must we entertain frustrations, difficulties, sorrows, unbearable pain, and the mystery of not understanding life? If God is good, why does he allow all of this suffering?

The questions the disciples asked Jesus often provide us with insight into their thinking. Acting as a mirror, their inquiries reflect the current thought of the day. Evidently there were many who felt that suffering was a direct result of sin, and that any time one suffered he did so because of some sin and only because of this. Thus, when the disciples witnessed Jesus showing compassion to a blind man, they posed this question: "Master, who did sin, this man, or his parents, that he was born blind?" (John 9:2).

The cynic would answer the disciples' question by asking another: What difference does it make? If a man is afflicted, who cares what caused it? Knowing whether or not it was his sin or the sin of his forefathers doesn't make any difference; he still hurts, doesn't he?

It is true that regardless of who caused it, the pain will still be there, but it is not true that the cause doesn't make a difference. It makes all the difference in the world.

Peter had much to say concerning suffering. The word appears some sixteen times in the five short chapters of his first epistle; it is the key word of the epistle. In these chapters he recognizes that there are many kinds of pain and that there is a common attitude toward it. He says:

> Finally, be ye all of one mind, having compassion one of another, love as brethren, be pitiful, be courteous: not rendering evil for evil, or railing for railing: but contrariwise blessing . . . . and be ready always to give an answer to every man that asketh you a reason of the hope that is in you with meekness and fear: having a good conscience; that, whereas they speak evil of you, as of evildoers, they may be ashamed that falsely accuse your good conversation in Christ. For it is better, if the will of God be so, that ye suffer for well doing, than for evil doing. For Christ also hath once suffered for sins, the just for the unjust, that he might bring us to God (1 Pet. 3:8–9, 15–18).

Suffering undeniably exists. It is something that each of us experiences at some turn of the road in life. Peter is not saying, as some would, that the evil man gets by without suffering in this world, that he has it easy. The fact that a man is evil does not mean that he will escape all suffering, for suffering is the lot of the human race and each of us will have to know some heartache.

Is he not saying, If there must be suffering, it is far better to suffer for well doing than for evil doing? Plainly enough he distinguishes between suffering as the consequence of sin and suffering for righteousness' sake. The righteous will suffer because they are apostles of God, believers in the Lord Jesus Christ.

Choice

The Bible offers various reasons for suffering. First, it is the result of our being members of a fallen race. God said unto man, Here is my will, my desire, my wish for your life. But man rebelled against God and chose sin. The serpent said to Eve, If you will do as I say, you will know things that you could not otherwise know. And it was true. One of those things that she experienced for the first time was pain.

There are some things that come to us as a result of belonging to the human race. This is not to say that all suffering is the result of the sins of Adam and Eve, but that as part of the family of man we daily choose sin instead of the righteousness of God.

Second, some suffering comes to man as a penalty for his own evil doing. When we defy the laws of God and common sense, suffering follows. Proverbs 5:22 says: "His own iniquities shall take the wicked himself, and he shall be holden with the cords of his sins."

Third, God tells us that suffering is a method of correction. Those whom God is concerned about, those whom he loves, he also corrects that he might shape them more perfectly according to his will (Heb. 12:6–11). "But when we are judged, we are chastened of the Lord, that

100

we should not be condemned with the world" (1 Cor. 11:32).

Fourth, we are allowed to suffer in order that we may learn to know the will of God and be better prepared to walk with him. Paul had a postgraduate course in suffering. No mortal suffered more than he. Yet in the last days of his life he was still saying, "Oh that I might know Christ, that I might know him in the fellowship of his suffering" (Phil. 3:8-10). We really do not understand how much God loves us until we know something about how much he suffered for us. We cannot fully understand the love of God until we know something about the fellowship of his suffering on Calvary.

Finally, the Scriptures teach that we suffer for the glory of God in order that people may know that his grace and strength are sufficient. In our living and dying, others should be conscious that God's grace will see us through the hour. Only the strong will be willing to suffer for Christ's sake, and all those who "live godly in Christ Jesus shall suffer persecution" (2 Tim. 3:12).

When suffering comes, we either become bitter or better because of it. But we ought to learn to live with it realistically. In the hills of Tennessee one of our preachers went hunting with a local lad. When the boy hurt his foot, the minister, realizing that because of the seriousness of the wound the boy must be in great pain, asked him what he was going to do about it. The boy replied, "Let it hurt."

We cannot handle suffering in a few moments. There always comes the awareness, the understanding, that there is nothing we can do about it—no way we can fathom it, no way we can understand it. Even if we could, it still wouldn't ease the pain. There are times when there is nothing one can do with suffering and sorrow except to put it on the throne of heaven and let it rest there until the depth of the wound burns itself out. Then, perhaps, we may find a clear picture of God's will.

Our attitude toward suffering is of far greater importance than the suffering itself. In World War II, a great many parents in London became anxious about getting their children out of the bombed city. Many of them had the opportunity to arrange for their children to go into the highlands of Scotland or to Ireland. After the war was over the mental and physical health of these children was compared to the health of those who stayed with their mothers and fathers during the crisis. As strange as it may seem, the doctor said that those who were rocked to sleep by their fathers and mothers, who felt the security of their love, had a far healthier attitude than those who were sent away to safety. Some problems within can be far greater than problems without.

An element in verse 17 of 1 Peter 3 haunts us. Peter says it is better to suffer for well doing than for evil doing—*if the will of God be so.* This phrase is one we are tempted to use as a catch-all for anything we can't explain, can't understand, or can't handle. Peter is saying, if the will of God be so, we should suffer. But let us not interpret everything as being the will of God. To know what is truly God's will should be man's highest quest.

The telephone rang and the sheriff's office told me that the sheriff would like to pick me up in front of the church; he had a tragic death message to deliver and would like for me to be with him. When he came, he told me that

102

he had just come from investigating an accident involving a young serviceman home from one of the wars. I went into the house and told the family the news as best I could. In an attempt to console them, another person who was present said, "Now, don't you worry about this. This is the will of God or it would never have happened."

But all things are not the will of God! It is not the will of God that men start wars! It is not the will of God that men bring sorrow into their own hearts and lives and nations! Some of our suffering we are responsible for because we have made wrong choices.

Conscience

Peter admonishes us to have a good conscience before God (1 Pet. 3:16).

What is conscience? It is the moral concept which God has put into man; and unless it has been completely destroyed, it can act as a radar system and be of invaluable help in all of man's moral decisions. It ought to be motivated by God. Romans 9:1 says that it is to be directed by the Spirit of God.

The result of a good conscience is good conversation. Have a good conscience, says Peter, that those who speak evil of you "may be ashamed that falsely accuse your good conversation in Christ." He is saying, Let your conscience, your conduct, and your conversation be such that they put to flight anything that men would say against you. Then, such gossip will be inconsistent with the living out of your days. The late Dr. George W. Truett lived such an exemplary life that at a testimonial dinner in his behalf, he was referred to as "the conscience of Dallas." Even Pilate admitted he could find no fault with Jesus Christ.

God's teachings emphasize the importance of influence and character. "A 'good conscience' implies a 'good conversion' in Christ," said F. B. Meyer. Everything we do reflects on our Master. The disciples realized the importance of the Christian's influence and looked for men "of good report" (1 Tim. 3:7; see also Acts 6:3). Such report is greatly to be prized by the believer.

A man's creed will determine his conduct. Often you hear someone brag that he never won a good-conduct medal. This isn't something to be proud of. When Saul was stricken by the voice of God on the road to Damascus, his creed changed and thereafter his conduct. Saul was no longer proud to be known as a persecutor of Christians.

Consequences

On the other hand, you as a Christian may be persecuted for your beliefs. You may suffer even when you are right before God. But if you let him, God will fight your battles for you. When your good conduct or character is maligned, remember the words of a great president: "Make no apology nor explanation for your behavior; your friends don't need it and your enemies won't believe you."

Joseph was mistreated by his own brothers, but God used their wrong for good. And when he was imprisoned for a sin he didn't commit because of someone's false report, again he came forth victorious. What can be worse than a man suffering in prison innocently, you ask? Only one thing—suffering in prison and being guilty. Man's first inescapable prison is the walls of his own life, the testimony of his own soul, the integrity of his own spirit. And if he suffers innocently, at least there is not the condemnation in his own heart. He can still live as a man and as a Christian.

Daniel was warned not to pray in public. But he went ahead and "gave thanks before his God, as he did aforetime" (Dan. 6:10). He suffered the consequences of his choice, but with God at his side. Likewise, when Daniel's three friends were put into the fiery furnace, there was a fourth man in the fire, appearing as the Son of God and protecting them.

Jehovah told the Hebrew children that they would pass through the fire but not be burned, pass through the waters but not be engulfed (see Isa. 43:2). The difference would be the presence of God, his companionship and company. Perhaps the reason God is not real to some of us is that we have never passed through the fire.

Job suffered. His friends came as foes, slyly giving him a chance to make his confession. "All right," they said to him, "if you want to get it off your chest, tell us about it. You know and we know that you wouldn't be suffering this way if you hadn't done something against God. Tell us about it and you will feel better." Where there is smoke, they thought to themselves, there must be fire. Job had nothing to say, and his suffering was made greater because of the misunderstanding of friends. There is little pain worse than this.

Then his wife came to him and said, "Job, I can't stand this much longer; why don't you just simply curse God and give it all up?" Old Job raised himself to his full spiritual height and said toward heaven, "Though he slay me, yet will I trust in him" (Job 13:15). Such a faith healed his heart. God reached down and touched his body and mind, and the restoration of Job is a picture of hope for every life.

We do not suffer alone. Jesus is our example. It is easier to suffer for righteousness if we remember that he who was just suffered for the ungodly.

There is value in suffering. It proves us, perfects us, preserves us, and purges us. Besides, such sufferings as we know on earth "are not worthy to be compared with the glory which shall be revealed in us" (Rom. 8:18). Christ suffered, and is the servant better than the master? We have only to be concerned that our own consciences do not accuse us. For it is better for the whole world to rise up against us than for God to be disappointed!

*"Being made so much better
than the angels, as he hath
by inheritance obtained a
more excellent name than
they" (Heb. 1:4).*

12

The Crowning of Christ

Only one man has perfectly pleased God—Jesus Christ.
In Hebrews 1:4 he is compared to angels and declared
to be "so much better than" they. A close examination of
this verse and passage reveals that it refers to the crowning of Christ as the one to whom "every knee should
bow" (Phil. 2:10).

When the Jewish writer of Hebrews declared that
Jesus Christ was the Son of God and was made better
than the angels, he was speaking from the context of
Jewish beliefs. Angels were very important in Jewish
thought.

The words translated "angel" in both Greek and
Hebrew mean "messenger." The angels are the highest
created beings, living ever with God, surrounding him
with worship and serving as his army and messengers to
men. Mankind and God being separated by sin, the
angels served as intermediaries, and the Jewish people

held them in high regard. The Old Testament as well as the New records frequent appearances of angels as messengers with a word from God.

The Book of Hebrews begins with a closely reasoned argument on the superiorities of Christ. He is better than the prophets; he is better than Moses, Aaron and Joshua; he is better than the angels. God's word through Jesus Christ is final and better than all other revelations, for Christ is God's Son, the "heir of all things" (Heb. 1:2).

We will look at Christ's crowning in the light of three stages in his life and ministry: (1) his clothing in earthly flesh, (2) his conduct in exacting flawlessness, and (3) his coronation in everlasting fame.

His Clothing in Earthly Flesh

Jesus was "made so much better than the angels." The word translated "being made" is not the Greek word normally translated "to make," that is, "to construct or fashion out of existing materials." Rather it is the same word used of the making of the universe, which means "to become." Concerning Christ, it refers to his clothing in earthly flesh.

We could, therefore, translate the beginning of the verse "having become so much better than the angels." We seem to have a contradiction here, a paradox. Jesus Christ was the Son of God—God himself. "I and my Father are one," he said; "he that hath seen me hath seen the Father" (John 10:30; 14:9). How would he ever need to *become* "better than the angels"?

We find the answer in the fact that he came to this

earth as a man—"the Word became flesh" (John 1:14, RSV). It was a willing sacrifice he made; the exalted Son of God came to earth as a lowly man. He was born as a baby of a virgin in Bethlehem, which was not her home, and his cradle was a manger because there was no room in the inn.

What did his becoming man involve? It meant that he became the servant instead of the sovereign. "Let this mind be in you, which was also in Christ Jesus," Paul wrote to his friends in Philippi (2:5). He, "though he was in the form of God, did not count equality with God a thing to be grasped [clung to], but emptied himself, taking the form of a servant, being born in the likeness of men" (Phil. 2:5-7, RSV). He became a lowly man, lower than the angels.

He gave up his glory; he set it aside. "I have glorified thee on the earth," he said in his prayer to his Father. "I have finished the work which thou gavest me to do. And now, O Father, glorify thou me with thine own self with the glory which I had with thee before the world was" (John 14:4-5).

He had to experience the humility of humanity. He left the pleasure and prosperity of heaven for the poverty of earth. "Foxes have holes, and birds of the air have nests," he told a would-be follower, "but the Son of man hath not where to lay his head" (Luke 9:58). To him the souls of men were worth more than all the wealth in the world.

Coming to earth clothed in flesh meant that Christ gave up the happiness of heaven for the heartaches of humanity. He experienced sorrow just as you and I do.

109

We see him standing outside the tomb of Lazarus, his beloved friend, weeping. He sacrificed the security of heaven to become involved in the sadnesses of this life. To see unrepentant men race toward doom in their sins grieved him greatly.

When Christ came to this earth in human flesh, he became lower than the angels. This does not mean that angels were superior to him in moral excellence, but rather that for a while they were above him in dignity and power. For our benefit he put these aside, because he loved us so much.

King Henry IV of France was visiting a certain village one day with some members of his court. At their approach, a very poor man bowed himself completely to the ground. The king responded by doing the same.

Those with him were astonished. One asked why he had condescended to return the salutation in like manner.

Quickly the king replied, "Would your king be excelled in politeness by one of the most lowly of his subjects?"

Christ was not willing that men, his subjects, should experience sorrow he did not share. He set aside all of his splendor and became like us, but he excelled us, because he lived the human life without sin. Only so could he "by himself purge our sins," and become again better than the angels (Heb. 1:3, 4).

His Conduct in Exacting Flawlessness

The verse in Hebrews goes on to say, "as he hath by inheritance obtained a more excellent name than they." Our prime interest centers in the words "by inheritance obtained." We need to look not only at the fact that Christ came to earth in flesh, but also at the way in which he lived that earthly life. We could call it his conduct in exacting flawlessness.

How did he obtain this more excellent name? He did it by living a perfect life. In a world filled with corruption, greed, and sin of every description, Jesus came and lived without sin. His life was characterized by qualities every man's life should have.

He was loving and compassionate. We can see this in his treatment of sinful women, his acceptance of despised tax-gatherers, his compassion on the sick and helpless. "Hereby perceive we the love of God, because he laid down his life for us" (1 John 3:6). Jesus' perfect life demonstrated godly love in the right attitude. It was for others more than for self. His love was not the sensual fleeting love which that term so often implies today. It was deep, sacrificial, self-giving love.

Jesus Christ was faced with temptations just as we are. We are prone to say, "Oh, it was easy for him. He was God!" But the writer of Hebrews says that "we have not a high priest who is unable to sympathize with our weaknesses, but one who in every respect has been tempted as we are, yet without sinning" (Heb. 4:15, RSV). Jesus recognizes and understands our testings because of his own personal experience.

His perfection also involved his humility. This is a tremendous characteristic to have and a most difficult one to achieve. It is chiefly a matter of putting others first. Jesus' own words reveal his humility: "The Son of man came not to be ministered unto, but to minister, and to give his life a ransom for many" (Matt. 20:28). Humility is not a sign of weakness; it is a characteristic of

111

strength. Our Lord displayed this in his unyielding yet compassionate righteousness.

As we think of the humility of Christ we are reminded of his meekness, also. Many people identify meekness with a "milk toast" kind of mildness. The English word "meek" loses much of the emphasis of the Greek word which it translates. Used of Christ and by Christ, it connotes a gentle strength. One of the best ways to illustrate it is by considering the horse. This animal has tremendous strength. He has power to burn, but in many cases it is raw, untamed power. It serves no real purpose. But if horse power is brought under control of harness or bridle, it is useful. It is channeled.

Meekness in a man is much like that. His strength and character have to be channeled to maximum good use. Christ was no weakling. He had a controlled strength that blessed and helped people. It built up and healed rather than abused or hurt. When he was abused by others, he loved them and tried to win them instead of striking back or getting even.

Christ's perfect life was also characterized by obedience. "And being found in fashion as a man, he humbled himself, and became obedient unto death, even the death of the cross" (Phil. 2:8). We are told that in Gethsemane "he went a little farther, and fell on his face, and prayed, saying, O my Father, if it be possible, let this cup pass from me: nevertheless not as I will, but as thou wilt" (Matt. 26:29).

His obedience centered in absolute devotion to his Father and his Father's will. It was not exemplified in aggressive determination, but rather by quiet willingness to accomplish the divine goal.

The perfect life of Jesus Christ made his crucifixion by sinful men the logical result. His obedience led him to the cross of Calvary. His sacrifice is spoken of many places in the Old Testament. "He was oppressed, and he was afflicted, yet he opened not his mouth: he is brought as a lamb to the slaughter, and as a sheep before her shearers is dumb, so he openeth not his mouth. He was taken from prison and from judgment: and who shall declare his generation? For he was cut off out of the land of the living: for the transgression of my people was he stricken" (Isa. 53:7-8).

In the New Testament he spoke of it himself: "And he began to teach them, that the Son of man must suffer many things, and be rejected of the elders, and of the chief priests, and scribes, and be killed, and after three days rise again" (Mark 8:31). Throughout his ministry his face was set toward the cross. He knew it was necessary. By sinning, man had severed fellowship with God, yet God loved man so much he wanted that fellowship restored. Jesus died as the sacrifice in order that sin might be atoned for; he was our perfect, sin-bearing Lamb.

In conversation with a Christian, a skeptic raised the standard objection to Christianity: "The church is full of hypocrites."

"That is very true," responded the Christian, "and I won't attempt to justify their failings. But I will challenge you to speak a word of criticism against Jesus Christ himself."

The skeptic was surprised and seemed almost frightened. "Well, no, I couldn't find fault with him. He was perfect."

"Exactly," replied the Christian. "That's why I was attracted to him—because I'm not like him at all, only a guilty sinner. And the evils practiced by some of his followers don't turn me away from him. My salvation hangs on what he has done, not on what they are doing."

His Coronation in Everlasting Fame

The writer of Hebrews goes on to say that Jesus was "made so much better than the angels, as he hath by inheritance obtained *a more excellent name than they.*" We will look at his coronation in everlasting fame by examining his excellence.

The word translated "more excellent" is not the same word which, earlier in the verse, was translated "better."

The first word has the idea of superiority. Here is included the idea of difference. As M. R. Vincent says, "The Son's name differs from that of the angels, and is more different for good." The remainder of Hebrews 1 tells how Jesus is different and more excellent than the angels.

We find first of all that the angels are his, they belong to him. Jesus himself talked about sending out his angels at the end of the world (Matt. 13:41, 24:31). Paul refers to the same time "when the Lord Jesus shall be revealed from heaven with his mighty angels" (2 Thess. 1:7). They are his servants, his ministers, his army. He is commander over them.

Another point in his excellence is that repentance and remission of sins are preached in his name. Jesus himself commanded this (Luke 24:47), and the early church ful-

114

filled his commission throughout the then known world. The church has continued to proclaim forgiveness of sin in the name of Jesus Christ, for there is salvation in no other name, "for there is none other name under heaven given among men, whereby we must be saved" (Acts 4:12). Jesus is Savior; no angel can claim that.

The name of Jesus is powerful. Mighty miracles have been performed in his name. Peter and John healed the man born lame in the name of Jesus at the Gate Beautiful of the Temple. As Peter said to him, "Silver and gold have I none; but such as I have give I thee; In the name of Jesus Christ of Nazareth rise up and walk." Then Peter "took him by the right hand, and lifted him up: and immediately his feet and ankle bones received strength" (Acts 3:6-7).

A part of the kingship of Christ is the worship he receives. Throughout the Gospels we find Jesus receiving the worship of people who came to him for help or in gratitude. His disciples worshiped Jesus after the resurrection (Matt. 28:9). Paul taught that one day everyone will worship Jesus Christ, bowing the knee to him (Phil. 2:10).

However, in Colossians 2:18 Paul warns against worship of angels. "Let no man beguile you of your reward in a voluntary humility and worshipping of angels, intruding into those things which he hath not seen, vainly puffed up by his fleshly mind." The angels are not to receive the worship which rightfully belongs to God alone.

Christ is more excellent than the angels because he is the recipient of their worship. They adore and praise him. "And again, when he bringeth in the firstbegotten into the world, he saith, And let all the angels of God worship him" (Heb. 1:6).

We see his greatness in the numerous names and titles he is given. It has been said that 208 different names are assigned to Jesus in the Bible. They range from Son of the Highest, Immanuel, the Word, and the Lamb of God to Messiah and the King of Israel.

"Wherefore God also hath highly exalted him, and given him a name which is above every name: That at the name of Jesus every knee should bow, of things in heaven, and things in earth, and things under the earth; and that every tongue should confess that Jesus Christ is Lord, to the glory of God the Father" (Phil. 2:9-11).

His truly is "a name above every name." He has been crowned King by God himself: "Yet have I set my king upon my holy hill of Zion" (Ps. 2:6). "And he hath on his vesture and on his thigh a name written, KING OF KINGS, AND LORD OF LORDS" (Rev. 19:16). He has been given the seat of honor at the right hand of the Father. He has an everlasting throne. These things cannot be said of any angel.

An outstanding Egyptian king of the second century named Ptolemy was an astronomer and mathematician. He decided to build a mammoth lighthouse and commissioned a man named Sostratus to design it. Called The Pharos, it later became one of the seven wonders of the world. As ruler, Ptolemy insisted that the structure should bear his inscription as a personal memorial. But Sostratus didn't think the king should get all the credit.

On the front of the lighthouse, in a thick plaster, Sostratus put the name and title of Ptolemy. It would be eye-catching at first, but later would be worn away by the elements. Secretly he cut his own name in the granite underneath.

For decades the sea dashed against the plaster and eroded it, though it lasted the lifetime of the monarch. Obliterated, it left the name "Sostratus" standing in bold relief! In the same way, worldly fame often disappears before the relentless waves of time.

After looking at Jesus, clothed in earthly flesh, conducting himself in exacting flawlessness, our eyes come finally to see him exalted by coronation in everlasting fame. His is an eternal name which shines above every name, even that of the angels—his is "a more excellent name" than theirs.

117

*"To be with Christ ... is
far better" (Phil. 1:23).*

13
Delightful Dilemma

We have been thinking about some comparatives of
Christianity. Sometimes the comparison has been, not
just between the good and the bad or the right and the
wrong, but often—and most difficult of all—between two
rights. The Bible says there are things to be sought which
are better than sacrifice, better than rubies, better than
the mighty, better than a brother, better than a stalled
ox, better than precious ointment, and better than laughter. We have also seen that it is better to enter life
maimed than to enter hell whole, better to die than to
have our glorying in Christ made void, better to suffer
for well doing than for evil doing.

Perhaps the greatest comparison, which is scarcely a
comparison at all, comes from the pen of Paul: "For to
me to live is Christ, and to die is gain. But if I live in the
flesh, this is the fruit of my labour: yet what I shall
choose I wot not. For I am in a strait betwixt two, having

a desire to depart, and to be with Christ; which is far better" (Phil. 1:21–23). In Greek this verse reads "far *more* better"—a triple comparative which our language does not have. But such construction points up even more clearly Paul's emphasis. It is his positive conviction that the best is, indeed, "yet to be": for "to die is gain."

Choice

Paul was a tentmaker by vocation and a missionary and preacher by the calling of God. He usually did not stay many days in the same place unless he was in jail. He was a sufferer for the gospel. Therefore, he is not a mystic speaking out of a dense dream, but a man in a dilemma, faced with a choice between desire and duty.

There are times when Paul uses illustrations from his experiences. He talks about folding his tent—his temporary lodging—and stealing away to be with Jesus. In another place he speaks of the desire in his heart to cut loose from the mooring, to pull up anchor, to leave the harbor to go and be with the Lord forever. This is his desire as he writes to the Philippians.

Paul says that he is in a strait between two choices, being pressured by both sides. "If I really let myself go, if I really do what I want to do, I will just turn loose and go on to be with Jesus," he says. But talking to the church at Philippi, he says, "I am pressured on the other side because of my need to be with you. You are young in the faith; you are not strong in the Word. There are temptations on every side, persecutions all about us; and it is more needful that I remain with you."

Actually, whichever choice Paul makes, the relationship

119

is a continuing one, for "to live is Christ" and to die is to be with with Christ. If he stays, he is with Christ's friends; if he goes, he is with Christ himself. Either way he doesn't change course. What detains him is his passion for his people. Besides, the choice is really up to God, whose appointments Paul accepts without murmur.

Confidence

A number of years ago a ship was built that was said to be unsinkable. Because men relied so much upon their ability they did not supply all the necessary safety measures. There were not enough lifeboats. In the early part of a Saturday evening on the ship's first voyage, you could hear the people aboard the *Titanic* singing as the band played "There'll Be a Hot Time in the Old Town Tonight." But in a little while the inevitable happened. Out on the Atlantic, they ran into an iceberg. As people were trying to scramble into the safety of the few lifeboats that were there, you could hear the same band playing, but a different tempo—a mournful sound. They were playing "Nearer, My God, to Thee." It was the same evening, the same ship, and the same band; the difference was made by the proximity of death. Many were now faced with the end of life, with going to be with the master whom they had served, whether God or Satan. With this prospect, their attitude changed altogether.

Not one of us really wishes to die. Many are terribly afraid of dying. But there is no reason to fear death if we actually believe and obey what the Bible says. Often we do not act as if we believe. We feel that death is an intruder spoiling our favorite plans. Death is that inevitable word that cancels out all the things we want to do. It may be dressed up and the outward appearance changed, but it is still our most terrible enemy.

We are changing a great many customs connected with funeral services as though that might alter the outcome. The morticians' magazine tells us that death is being dressed up, that colors are worn more instead of the traditional black of mourning. But changing one's dress doesn't change the inevitable. We may try to disguise it, but death remains our robber.

There are many conflicting ideas about death. Many people say, "We can't know anything about the future life, so death holds nothing but darkness and mystery for us." They bury their heads in the sand and refuse to listen to the gospel of hope. But even though they may refuse again and again to listen to any words from a man, they cannot refuse to listen to the voice of God or the voice of death that taps each person on the shoulder.

Paul recognized that death held a terror for the Hebrew people. They were frightened of going to the grave, of the dark unknown, of being unclothed, of not knowing what the eternal body would be like. Paul therefore, being a Hebrew among Hebrews, said to them, "I would not have you to be ignorant, brethren, concerning them which are asleep, that ye sorrow not, even as others which have no hope" (1 Thess. 4:13).

It is natural that we sorrow in the face of death because we have viewed death on this side with paleness and finality. Paul says nothing about our not sorrowing, but says that our sorrow ought to be tempered with the hope we have which is in Christ Jesus. We suffer, but not as those who have no hope; for if we believe that Jesus died and rose again, then we have hope within us. And we ought to be able to give evidence of that hope.

Besides, when we lose a loved one it is really for ourselves that we weep, saying, "What shall I do without him?" But we shouldn't weep for the Christian dying; after all, he isn't asking what he will do without us, for he is going to be with Christ! As the real test of metal is the acid and the fire, so the real test of religion is in living and dying. Does your religion support your soul in sorrow?

Paul says that death is the last enemy. It is the enemy that came into the world because of Adam and Eve's choice to sin, and it is the enemy that Christ came to destroy. Enemy? Paul said that

> when this corruptible shall have put on incorruption, and this mortal shall have put on immortality, then shall be brought to pass the saying that is written, Death is swallowed up in victory. O death, where is thy sting? O grave, where is thy victory? The sting of death is sin; and the strength of sin is the law. But thanks be to God, which giveth us the victory through our Lord Jesus Christ (1 Cor. 15:54-57).

On resurrection morning when the shout of the archangel of God shall come, and the graves shall be opened and those who are dead shall be raised, with one foot in heaven and the other on earth we shall be able to say, "O death, where is thy sting? O grave, where is thy victory? God has conquered all." Death is the last enemy, and one day its defeat will be a victorious thing in our own sight. We have already been staked out and claimed by the Lord.

Paul has confidence. There is confidence in his preaching. There is confidence in his belief. There is confidence in all that he says; it echoes and reechoes throughout the Scriptures. In 2 Timothy 1:12 you hear him say, "I know whom I have believed, and am persuaded that he is able to keep that which I have committed unto him against that day." And in Romans 8:28: "We know that all things work together for good to them that love God, to them who are the called according to his purpose." Then we hear him as he speaks in 2 Corinthians 5:1: "We know that if our earthly house of this tabernacle were dissolved, we have a building of God, an house not made with hands, eternal in the heavens." Paul said these are the things we can believe. These are the things which will sustain us when we are dying. This is the confidence of God.

To many, life means fun, fame, and fortune. But this world had lost its charm for Paul because his concept of living was entirely centered on Christ. His attainments couldn't be listed in the January inventories nor counted in the bank vaults of some large city. But his achievements made it easy for him to sleep at night, and he looked forward to the eternal rest promised the children of God in Hebrews 4:9. He was confident that he would hear the "well done" of the Father. While in the Appian Way prison, he reflects on his life: "I have fought a good fight, I have finished my course, I have kept the faith: henceforth, there is laid up for me a crown of righteousness" (2 Tim. 4:7–8). There is humility in his voice and confidence in his heart.

Job finally came through his dark days. His body was a mess of sores, and he had endured the added anxiety of the misunderstanding of his friends and his wife. He felt he would not live long. He covered himself with the ashes of mourning and, as though he were dying, yet with the confidence of an undying man, he said, "I know that my redeemer liveth, and that he shall stand at the latter day upon the earth" (Job 19:25).

Jesus, having died upon the cross, was put into the tomb and his enemies sealed it, rolling a stone in front of the entrance and guarding it day and night. In spite of their preparations, Jesus laid aside his graveclothes and came out to walk forty days before men. He removed the sting of death and the grave.

The confidence of the Christian can be sure and real. It is complete and continuing—we have God's word for it.

Comparisons

"My desire," Paul said, "is to be with Christ, which is far better."

If only we could come to a full realization that heaven is indeed far better! We need to know that it is greater than anything we can imagine. "Eye hath not seen, nor ear heard, neither have entered into the heart of man, the things which God hath prepared for them that love him" (1 Cor. 2:9). Great planners of human society have visualized utopias on earth, but none can fathom what God has prepared. Jesus had cautioned the disciples that there was no place on earth for them to rest: "The foxes have holes, and the birds of the air have nests; but the Son of man hath not where to lay his head" (Matt. 8:20). But he promised toward the end that when they had finished their earthly tasks, a home in heaven would await them: "I go to prepare a place for you. And . . . I will come again, and receive you unto myself; that where I am, there ye may be also" (John 14:2–3).

Doubtless all of us have questions about the afterlife, and the Bible does give us some answers.

What is heaven? Most of us think heaven is a kind of glorified old-age home where people go when they get too old to do anything else. Heaven isn't very real to many of us. It is not a very glorious place; we do not sing of it as a joy. I think the greatest statement I ever heard said concerning heaven came from the mouth of a child. When our little girl died, one of her playmates said, "She's luckier than we are. She got to go to heaven first." Heaven is the last place most of us want to go. It's not real to us. But to Paul heaven was real, heaven was home, heaven was glorious, heaven was God.

When do we go to heaven? Just as soon as we die. When do we get to be with Jesus? As soon as we die. The body is placed reverently in the earth, but the spirit goes home to God who created it. A minister once said to a group of young pallbearers as they carelessly handled the body of their friend in the casket, "Young men, tread softly; you carry the temple of the Holy Spirit in that box." We reverence the body. We lay it to rest. It is a chariot that is worn out. It is an envelope that has served its purpose. It is a case which has been used. It is laid down and the soul, the personality, the person has gone home to be with God. It is just that simple. Paul said, "In the body I am with you, and out of this body I am with Jesus." It's just that simple. In the body I am with you, but simultaneously, instantaneously, at the same moment the spirit ceases to breathe, the spirit leaves to be with Christ.

Where is heaven? There are some who would say that

125

heaven is in the north, and they feel there is reason for thinking this. But there are three heavens mentioned in the Bible: the heaven where the birds fly, the second heaven where the stars are put into place, and the third heaven where God dwells. But upon all the authority of the Scriptures, heaven is where Jesus is, and this is heaven enough.

The Bible says that "we shall see him as he is" (1 John 3:2). "For now we see through a glass, darkly; but then face to face: now we know in part," but then we shall have perfect and complete knowledge of ourselves, of Jesus Christ, and of heaven (1 Cor. 13:12).

What shall we be like? The verse in 1 John also says, "We shall be like him." This is the strangest, most wonderful thing about heaven—being like Jesus. Here on earth we have been born again. We have tried to copy his works. We have tried to walk as he walked, talk as he talked, pray as he prayed. But still, as we lie down to sleep at night, we find that we have fallen far short of all that Jesus wants. But when we get out of this body and lay it aside, then we shall be like him. Oh, glorious day! Then we won't have to apologize any more. We won't have to say "I'm sorry" any more. We won't have to confess our sins any more. We won't have to correct our faults, clean up our mistakes any more. Then we shall be like him and have perfect peace.

Will we know one another in heaven? The Bible tells us that we shall be with Jesus, and have perfect fellowship with God and the saints. Our loved ones will be there, and we will know them. There won't be any reception line which we shall have to go through to be introduced. We were given a preview of this on the

Mount of Transfiguration. Peter, James, and John were there with Jesus, and heaven came down. Moses and Elijah appeared, and Jesus didn't say, "Peter, this is Moses." They knew each other. Everything that is taught in the Bible assures that we shall know each other in heaven.

When someone asked Dwight L. Moody at a funeral service, "Mr. Moody, will we know each other in heaven?" Mr. Moody replied, "Don't you think we will have as much sense in heaven as we do on earth?" Of course we shall know each other in heaven.

What is heaven? Paul said there is not anything like it here. It cannot be compared with anything. Fourteen years earlier he had known a man who was "caught up into· paradise, and heard unspeakable words, which it is not lawful for a man to utter" (2 Cor. 12:4). He could say, though, that Jesus would return with a victorious shout to take his church to be with him.

The Book of Revelation gives us the clearest picture of heaven. There God's children "shall hunger no more, neither thirst any more; neither shall the sun light on them, nor any heat. For the Lamb which is in the midst of the throne shall feed them, and shall lead them unto living fountains of waters" (Rev. 7:16–17). And farther on the writer tells us, "God shall wipe away all tears from their eyes; and there shall be no more death, neither sorrow, nor crying, neither shall there be any more pain" (21:4). No more thirst, hunger, or pain, but only the choirs of heaven playing the harps of God. Could one ask for anything more?

Alfred Tennyson, the English poet, went to a funeral. Deeply touched at the going of his friend, he came back and sat down at a cluttered desk that he allowed no one to touch. His housekeeper, who had been in the home for a long while, saw that he was in a somber mood. She said, "Mr. Tennyson, you've written many things eloquently and well, but you've never voiced anything about death. How do you feel about death?" And as the shadows began to fall that October evening, Lord Tennyson, pen in hand, wrote these words:

> Sunset and evening star,
>   And one clear call for me!
> And may there be no moaning of the bar,
>   When I put out to sea,
>
> But such a tide as moving seems asleep,
>   Too full for sound and foam,
> When that which drew from out the boundless deep
>   Turns again home.
>
> Twilight and evening bell,
>   And after that the dark!
> And may there be no sadness of farewell,
>   When I embark;
>
> For though from out our bourne of Time and Place,
>   The flood may bear me far,
> I hope to see my Pilot face to face,
>   When I have crossed the bar.

Paul's words are seldom used except for funerals because theirs is a majestic music which we are not really in tune with. He was longing for the full consummation of his commission with the Master. To him death wasn't pathetic but a promotion; he couldn't see the gloom of the grave for the glory beyond.

DATE DUE
